TIL HEALING COMES

KEN DIGNAN

*A Closer Look at Divine Healing,
The Problem of Suffering,
And the Blessings of Redemption*

Copyright © 1993 by Ken Dignan

All rights reserved
Printed in the United States of America
International Standard Book Number: 1-883928-00-1
Library of Congress Catalog Card Number: 93-79314

Unless otherwise noted, all Scripture quotations are taken from the *Holy Bible, New International Version.* NIV®. Copyright © 1973, 1978, 1984 by International Bible Society. Used by permission of Zondervan Publishing House. All rights reserved. Personal emphasis, noted by italics, has also been added in various verses.

This book or parts thereof may not be reproduced in any form without permission of the author.

Published by:
Longwood Communications
397 Kingslake Drive
DeBary, FL 32713
904-774-1991

First Printing 1993
Second Printing 1996

Contents

Acknowledgments 5
Introduction: From Polio to Praise 8
I. God Is in Charge..18
II. God's Will and Healing 35
III. The Tension: Now and Not Yet 54
IV. Understanding Prayer, Faith and Miracles 77
V. Positioning Yourself for a Miracle 101
VI. Seasons of Suffering.................................112
VII. God Uses Handicaps.................................120
VIII. Serving Christ: More Than Healing 129
IX. The Best Is Yet to Come...........................141
Notes...154
Selected Bibliography 159
About the Author....................................162

'Til Healing Comes

Acknowledgments

Multitudes of books are available on the topic of healing. Many of them are helpful. But many books also bring much confusion to the subject.

While I recognize the tremendous diversity of thought on healing and miracles for today, I also know that well-meaning Christian people teach and preach all sorts of conflicting theories on healing and how to be healed. I believe we can come to a balance regarding this issue.

One major purpose of this book is to give a viewpoint on the Bible and healing through the eyes of a minister who has been educated and trained in the schools of a Pentecostal fellowship, the Assemblies of God, and who has been handicapped as the result of polio. Seeing the doctrine of healing through the eyes of someone who has a physical handicap and deformity can shed new light on this controversial subject.

I am an ordained minister with a Bachelor of Arts in Bible and pastoral studies from North Central Bible College, Minneapolis, Minnesota (1975) and a Master of Arts degree in biblical studies from the Assemblies of God Theological Seminary, Springfield, Missouri (1976).

I have been involved in full-time ministry in a number of Assemblies of God churches. I served at two churches as a youth pastor and became a senior pastor of Living Water Assembly of God in Bolingbrook, Illinois, a suburb of Chicago, in 1981. I was the pastor at Living Water until 1991. Currently I am the founder and president of 'Til Healing Comes Ministries and serve on the pastoral staff of a local church.

A preacher and teacher of God's Word, I have dedicated myself to studying and proclaiming it with all of my heart. I pray that this book will be an encouragement to the whole body of Christ, regardless of the denomination, adding insight to what the Bible reveals about God, healing, and suffering.

I have come to know a loving and personal God who is everything to me. Even in the midst of pain and difficulty He is far beyond what our human minds can comprehend.

This book is dedicated in love and appreciation to all those who have influenced my life: my wife, Joni; my four sons, Andy, Patrick, Ryan and Britt; my parents, Leo and Rosemary Dignan; my five brothers and two sisters in the Dignan clan; my pastor, Owen Carr; and the many Christian friends I have met along the way.

Acknowledgments

I would like to give a special word of appreciation to Joni Dignan, Gloria Smith and Marilyn Plantinga for typing and editing my manuscript.

This book is also dedicated to the many physically and mentally handicapped people of the world who still need hope and a vibrant relationship with the Lord and Savior Jesus Christ as they wait— *'Til Healing Comes.*

Introduction

FROM POLIO TO PRAISE

I was born on July 31, 1951, as a perfectly healthy baby boy. I began walking at the age of nine months. My father remembers that I could throw a small football right at his belt buckle. I was his firstborn, and I am sure he had his visions of my becoming an all-star football player, being an avid fan himself. My parents were as proud and happy as they could be.

When I was fourteen months old, they took me to an early fall picnic. Shortly thereafter I began to run a very high fever, accompanied with vomiting. Motionless and limp, I couldn't move my arms or legs at all, like a helpless rag doll. I was rushed to the hospital. My father recalls that as I was being wheeled away on the gurney, I whispered faintly, "My ball, my

Introduction

ball!"

Little did anyone know then that after this day, I'd never become my father's football player.

After a number of tests were performed, the results came back. The verdict was given to my fear-stricken parents: "Your son has polio." The disease left me paralyzed for awhile from the neck down, although I did not require the assistance of an iron lung. Eventually I was out of the contagious stage and slowly began to discover which muscles in my body were affected by the virus.

Next began the long hard road of rehabilitation. I was given two leg braces to support my weight so I could walk. My high chair was equipped with springs to assist my weak, almost motionless arms to bring a spoon to my mouth. God gave me parents who refused to give up or back down in the rehabilitation process. They begged, pleaded, bribed and ordered me to practice walking and other physical activities.

Much of what happened in those years from ages two to seven are a blur for me, with snatches of memory only here and there. They were traumatic years [obscured] learned together to dea[obscured]

bo[obscured] y brother Steve was [obscured] ther Ray joined the far[obscured] ith a total of nine chi[obscured]

be[obscured] six major surgeries [obscured]. Those were trying tin[obscured] ed the fears of pre- su[obscured] y, casts and stitches.

[obscured] what it meant to go th[obscured] andicaps. Some have sa[obscured] were born four years to[obscured] Salk vaccine which came out in 1955 and virtually stopped polio in its tracks. I could have agreed and lived a life of self-pity and anger. But with my God-given parents, I decided that I would make the best of what I had instead of longing for what I didn't have. I couldn't turn back the clock, no matter how hard I wished.

The cliches are easy to say, but sometimes difficult to put into practice: "It could have been worse," or "If life gives you a lemon, make lemonade," or "You can become bitter or better." Oh, I tried, but I continually fell short.

Let me digress here. If I were to use one word to describe someone who is handicapped, it might be frustrated. The extra inconveniences cause times of great aggravation. I describe them not to gain sympathy or to complain, but so that other handicapped people can identify with me, and so that those without handicaps can gain insight into the struggles involved.

I've never been able to dress myself. It's humbling to be dependent on someone else to pull up your pants, button your shirt, tie your shoes and put on your tie. For that matter, I can't get up whenever I want to. I have to depend on others to help me, so I am often dependent on their schedules.

Could you imagine not having the luxury of putting your hands in your pockets if you want to? I used to have my wallet placed in my back pocket in the morning. It became rather embarrassing, not to mention inconvenient, when buying something at a store to have to ask the clerk to reach into my pocket to retrieve it. Whenever I drop something on the floor, I cannot pick it up. I just hope someone is nearby to help me.

It is awkward not being able to take care of my personal toiletries on my own. I have some tools that

Introduction

give me assistance, but I still need help. It becomes a problem when I am away from anyone who can assist me in this personal necessity. In desperation I've often had to ask strangers to help me. But most of the time I just wait until I get home. That can be painful and difficult.

I cannot get up from a chair, nor can I climb stairs without assistance. When I fall, I cannot get up by myself and have to lie there helplessly until someone comes. Yes, growing up with a physical handicap was very hard. It was emotionally stressful to have to cope regularly with stares and constant questions of "What happened to you?" and "Why does your arm or leg look like that?"

Not being able to run, ride a bicycle, go swimming, play little league, climb trees, play on the playground—all saddened me. I tried to do things like the other kids, but got injured in the process. Frequently, I fell and cut my head, occasionally requiring stitches.

Amazingly enough, I would never quit, even if it meant danger and possible injury. My friends let me play in the neighborhood baseball games as a designated hitter. I sat on a stool as they pitched the ball to me. I was the only one on the team with a pinch runner and a pinch fielder.

As I grew older it became increasingly difficult to feel accepted by others. As the criteria for acceptance became more stringent, i.e., physical prowess and physique, I was left out more and more. In grade school I often stayed in the classroom during recess. I gloomily spent the hour wondering why this had happened to me.

A Musical Hippie

I developed a passion for music during my high school years, my role models being the Beatles and similar groups. The kitchen table, plates, a knife and a fork were my first "drum set." Eventually, I convinced my father to buy me a real set. To everyone's amazement, I could play. I had a natural beat. That led me into garage bands, sock hops and teen concert engagements. I was thrilled to finally do something as well as a "normal" person.

Although I had attended a normal grade school, I entered a high school for the handicapped because of the problem of accessibility. For the first time I was brought face to face with hundreds of physically handicapped and deformed children. Here I had to learn to accept my handicap.

I poured myself into music, practicing with the other musicians day after day. I ate, slept and breathed music. My friends and I went to numerous concerts: The Who, Santana, Led Zeppelin, Jethro Tull, Jimi Hendrix and many more. That was my entrance into the hippie culture. I became a "flower child," complete with long hair, denim and the party scene.

In college the attraction to music grew even greater. I wanted to go full-time into music and hoped one day to make it to the top. I quit college after a year and pursued music wholeheartedly. Little did I know what was around the corner.

Search for God

Life became more difficult. At 19 years old, I felt my life was falling apart. Helpless, hopeless and hurting, I turned to God for answers. I had faithfully attended church all my life, but did not know God personally. I cried out to Him the best way I knew how.

Introduction

He responded, as He always does. He put people in my path who told me about His love for me.

At that time in the 1970s, many people who were disillusioned with the hippie scene and party life were becoming Christians. These "Jesus freaks" became as turned-on for God as they had been turned-on to the sin of this world. A few new converts who attended the Stone Church of Palos Heights, Illinois, began to pray for me. Some came to visit me at my home. They told me about Jesus Christ, how He loved me, died for me and would become my personal Savior and Lord. They said I could actually know for sure I was going to heaven. I remember thinking, "This is too good to be true." I had always believed in God and the Bible, but never read it for myself.

I began attending their Bible studies and was totally changed as I gave my life to Jesus Christ. When I met Him as a Person, my spiritual eyes were opened. Suddenly I received a renewed strength and power to go on. No, my body was not changed. I still had a physical deformity, but I experienced Jesus' love that accepted me the way I was. The only requirement was that I give Him my heart and life. I became whole in Him. I went from polio to praise.

Here I was, filled with joy at my newfound relationship with God. I poured myself into Bible study, prayer and church meetings. I attended a church service or Bible study every night of the week. I knew now that the Lord loved me. People at this wonderful church loved me. I was basking in this unbelievable blessing from the Lord.

This Thing Called Healing

But, wait a minute. "Ken, you are crippled. You have a diseased body. You must get healed."

"Fine," I thought. I happened to attend a Pentecostal church that believed in healing for today. They practiced anointing the sick with oil according to James 5:14-15: "Is any one of you sick? He should call the elders of the church to pray over him and anoint him with oil in the name of the Lord. And the prayer offered in faith will make the sick person well; the Lord will raise him up. If he has sinned, he will be forgiven."

I believed with the best of them, yet nothing happened outwardly. I still had a deformed right hand. I had scoliosis. I needed a leg brace on my left leg.

Some people told me, "You need to claim your healing before you can get it. You need to confess it into existence before it happens. That's faith." Remember Hebrews 11:1? "Now faith is being sure of what we hope for and certain of what we do not see." Remember Mark 11:24? "Therefore I tell you, whatever you ask for in prayer, believe that you have received it, and it will be yours." You have to believe and act on it before you get it, they said.

I studied booklets written by numerous healing evangelists and pored over every book I could find that related to the subject. Practicing what I learned, I named my healing. I claimed my healing. I confessed my healing. I was earnest. I was sincere and genuinely open to God. Still nothing happened, but I kept on believing.

One day I thought, "If I'm going to get healed, I'd better act on my faith and confession." I took off my leg brace and said, "I'm healed." I didn't feel it, I didn't see it, but by faith I had it. Now I felt accepted. I felt no one would judge me for lack of faith. My Christian friends said, "That's it, Ken! Now you're living by faith." A couple of days later I was hobbling around, believing any day I'd wake up and my leg would be whole. On a Sunday evening after church I

Introduction

came home with some friends. As I was standing in the kitchen my leg gave out. All of my weight fell on it, and the bone fractured.

Oh, no! What had I done wrong now? Here I was telling everyone I was healed, and this happened. What was everyone thinking?

I had been happy just being saved. I was enjoying studying the Bible, praying and sharing my faith. Then I had to deal with this healing thing. Did I have doubt? Did a demon knock me over? Did I have a lack of faith? Did I claim the Word enough? All of these thoughts raced through my mind.

I had been a believer for only three or four months, and here I was in a cast and in the hospital. After three months it was taken off. But my friends and I were convinced that God wanted to heal me and that if I put my leg brace back on, I would be admitting defeat and thus giving the devil a victory. I kept the brace off and hobbled around for another couple of weeks, confessing my healing.

In pursuit of my desire to attend a Bible college, one weekend I went to College Days at North Central Bible College in Minneapolis, Minnesota. It was painful and scary to walk without the brace. I was standing out in front of an ice cream parlor, and the next thing I knew I was on the ground. My leg had given out again, and I had fallen on it. The ambulance took me to the hospital. The doctors put another cast on my twice-broken leg. The next day I had a long ride to Chicago in the back seat of a car.

God began to get through to me. He told me in my heart that He loved me. He told me I couldn't heal myself or force His hand. He let me know He had a plan for my life and I didn't have to get healed before He could use me. A weight lifted off my shoulders. What a hard way to learn a lesson!

You might say that I was stupid, or that I didn t have enough faith, or, perhaps, that I wasn't spiritually mature enough to attempt such a great miracle. But I was just trying to be open to a healing.

I came to realize that I could not put God in a box, that I could not come up with the exact confessions that would guarantee a healing. There is much more to the healing doctrine of God than mere formulas. There is God's sovereignty, God's timing, God's purpose, God's will, Satan's tricks, man's impatience, sin and so on. Healing can't be put in a nice, neat little package.

Through it all, the hand of God kept pushing me on. It would have been much easier to take a less demanding road, but God prompted me to go for it all: Bible college, seminary, marriage, four children, full-time ministry. These things are challenges for any physically capable person. God's grace and power are definitely sufficient.

I don't want my handicap to interfere with my dreams, goals and ambitions. Yet, though I do not like to admit it, there are times of frustration. And, yes, times of tears. Like any other happily married man, I would like to take a late-night walk with my wife, hand-in-hand or arm-in-arm. I would like to run, jump and frolic at the park with my boys—all four of them. I love sports very much, but, try as I might, I am forced to be a sideline fan. The closest I've gotten to real action is coaching my children's baseball teams and my church basketball teams. I dream what it would be like to swim or wrestle with my boys.

Through all the frustrations, though, I am thankful to God for my wife, my children, my brothers and sisters, and my parents. They are never annoyed at my handicap and are very supportive and loving. My children have never viewed me as a "cripple." They have the utmost respect and admiration for me. Once

Introduction

my son Patrick was asked by a neighbor why his father was crippled, and he answered with indignation, "He's not a cripple!" In his eyes, his dad could do anything.

I am very thankful for the grace of God and for the promise that either here through a miraculous healing, or when I get to heaven, I will be able to run, jump and smack a home run over the fence. All the inconveniences in my life cannot take away the joy of that promise.

Yes, I went from polio to praise. But along with my praise to God for His wonderful gift of new life, many questions still lingered about healing. In the chapters that follow I wish to take you on a journey through the Bible and share the insights and truths I've gained that assist me to live productively, joyfully and peacefully *'til healing comes.*

Chapter I

GOD IS IN CHARGE

Is God sovereign enough to decide who gets healed and who doesn't? The answer is a resounding "yes." But this answer must be qualified with a statement that says, "Yes, it is God's will to heal the sicknesses human beings experience because of sin. But experiencing healing, apart from the guarantee all believers have to receive a perfect body in future glory, is different for each of God's people. God reserves the right to decide who, when, where and how His children will receive various healings in this present life."

The Scriptures clearly teach us that God is in control of human affairs, including calamity and adversity. That God allows some to suffer great tragedy for a season is seen in Job. Paul's thorn in the flesh shows that God allows some to suffer for an extended period of time. That God allows some to receive miraculous healings is seen throughout Scripture, especially in the Gospels and Acts. Yet God is still God, and He has placed in the doctrine of healing a balance between His sovereignty and the accomplishing of His will by the prayers of His children. God always reserves the right to the last word.

Scripture Must Interpret Scripture

Those who use Scripture to fit into their own interpretation of healing, miracles and prosperity live dangerously on the brink of the misinterpretation of Scripture and false doctrine. Scripture must always interpret Scripture. To build a doctrine around certain passages of Scripture apart from the whole Bible is wrong and will mislead many sincere believers to arrive at erroneous conclusions about God and His will. For example, to say 3 John 2 is a word from the mouth of God for each and every believer is stretching the truth: "Dear friend, I pray that you may enjoy good health and that all may go well with you, even as your soul is getting along well." This is a wish, a greeting, a desire of goodwill from John for his friend. It was a standard greeting of the day. Something like, "How are you? I hope all is well and you are doing fine." It is in no way an ultimate statement from God, describing His divine will for every believer. Scripture must be interpreted contextually, historically, grammatically and theologically. If it is not, we can get God's will and His Word to say almost anything we want it to.

It is stretching Scripture to say that Psalm 105, which expressed God's will to keep all the Jews in the wilderness in divine health, expresses His will for every child of God throughout the ages. This is like saying that because God fed some people with quail and manna, believers should quit grocery shopping and claim that it is God's will for them to receive their own personal delivery of manna from heaven every day. This, of course, is ludicrous. Many promises recorded in Scripture were meant by God for a specific people during a specific time period for a specific purpose. You cannot hold God to them for all the ages. What He said and did to the people of Israel in the Old Testament was, in most cases, for them specifically. For example, we cannot apply Numbers 21:9 to contemporary situations. It is incorrect Bible intepretation to claim that all the sick who behold the cross will be healed just as the Jews who beheld the serpent lifted up by Moses were healed. It is also inaccurate to say the blessings and cursings of Deuteronomy 28 are applicable and true today for every believer. These were spoken to Israel for that time and for particular purposes. Who today believes it is Gods will for every Christian to experience the blessing of having ten children and an increase in his livestock (Deut. 28:4)?

If everything God said and taught in the Old Testament was His will forever, why doesn't the church practice everything in the Old Testament law, such as the laws regulating food, sacrifices and feast days? God's Word and His will must be interpreted correctly with a sound biblical framework.

You Need Accurate Theology to Determine God's Will

An individual believer equipped only with a Bible and the aid of the Holy Spirit is powerful and able to receive all that is necessary for salvation and eternal life. Bible study will reward that believer with fulfillment. But Bible study alone cannot result in an in-depth and accurate theology. Without the aid of biblical scholarship (languages, history, theology, hermeneutics), Bible study may even lead to error and false interpretation of Scripture. The church and individual believers need the assistance of orthodox Christian theology that comes to us through the ages. We need the help of current teachers and scholars to assist us in knowing the full counsel of God.

Even though there may be differences of opinion and interpretation, still there is in orthodox Christian teaching a thread of commonality that is true to the inspiration of Scripture, the deity of Christ, the Trinity, God's sovereignty and will, and the perseverance of the saints. Believers need an accurate theology to determine God's will for their lives.

When considering the sovereignty of God, it is fatalistic to believe that God does whatever He wants to at all times and that whatever He predetermines will happen—no matter what the believer does. This is dangerous because it tends to deny the believer's responsibility to use the authority, given in Jesus' name, to intercede and change troublesome circumstances. God doesn't want His children to roll over and play dead when bad things happen, thus accepting everything as God's will. God leaves room in many situations to allow the saints to exercise faith and authority in Christ to pray and make a difference. James 4:2 reveals, "You do not have, because you do not ask God." We are told throughout Scripture to ask. Matthew 7:7 tells us to "Ask and it will be given to you."

Various churches and denominations teach that God stopped healing people after the Bible was completed at the end of the first century. They teach that God allowed miracles during the time of Christ so all would believe He was the Messiah. They say that miracles took place during the founding of the early church to establish it as the work of God. They believe that, after the New Testament canon was established in the early 300s A.D., there was no longer a need for miracles and healing. God's Word does not teach this. The New Testament teaches that miracles should be expected in the church throughout the ages.

Paul reminded the Corinthian believers that they did not lack any spiritual gift as they eagerly waited for the Lord Jesus Christ to be revealed (1 Cor. 1:7). Though much of the New Testament had been written by the time Paul made it to Rome somewhere in 60–63 A.D., we see at the conclusion of Acts that God allowed Paul to minister healing to a whole island of people (Acts 28:7–10).

The book of James gives guidelines to be followed throughout the church age: "Is any one of you sick? He should call the elders of the church to pray over him and anoint him with oil in the name of the Lord. And the prayer offered in faith will make the sick person well; the Lord will raise him up" (James 5:14-15). God must be allowed to have the final say in all things, even healing. A theology that says it is God's desire that every believer get healed and never have to suffer physically is just as limited as a theology which says God does not heal today. God's Word teaches that He can sovereignly allow someone never to get sick; give another a miraculous healing without even a prayer; expect yet another to exercise faith and intercession to receive a healing; or even choose one not to be healed. We must allow God the power of sovereignty, yet we must also allow human beings to act responsibly and practice the discipline of prayer and faith. I believe that in the book of Acts, some healings and deliverances from demons could not have taken place if the disciples had not acted aggressively and stepped out in faith boldly, speaking the name of Jesus Christ over needy souls.

A Balanced Theology

We need an eclectic theology that balances the sovereignty of God with the authority given the church to break into the kingdom of darkness. God is God, and there are definitely secret things that belong to Him, unknowable to the child of God (Deut. 29:29). His thoughts are not our thoughts, as His ways are not our ways (Is. 55:8-9). The child of God must rest securely in the hands of God. He must stay close enough to Him to be able to discern what in the realm of His permissiveness can be changed by prayer and faith. God has shown openness to change in certain times of trial. Consider Abraham and the destruction of Sodom and Gomorrah (Gen. 19), Moses and the plagues of death on Israel (Num. 11) and King Hezekiah's pleading with God to give more years of life after He said it was his time to die (Is. 38:1-5).

There had to be some latitude given by God for faith and intercession to change situations that would otherwise go on the same and even be interpreted as His sovereign will. Theology in this case cannot be cut and dried.

There is so much confusion among many interpretations of the Bible because scholars can gather numerous scriptures to back up their own conclusions. One can say that at times God is Calvinistic, and at other times he is Arminian.[1] To put it simply, God is a God of predestination and sovereignty, but He is open to the free will and response of mere humans. It's not that God is schizophrenic or can't make up His mind. The truth is that God is on such a higher plane than we humans that we can only grasp Him as He is revealed in an abundance of experiences depicted in the Bible. It is very difficult to try to hold God down to a systematic theology by assembling various scriptures and saying, "This is how God is. Period."

God can do things that go beyond, but not contrary to, the revelation of Scripture. For instance, the book of Acts shows some phenomenal things occurring beyond understanding (Peter's shadow healing, Acts 5:15; Philip being transported by the Spirit to the Gaza Road, Acts 8:39; and Paul's healing through the handkerchiefs, Acts 19:11-12). Acts 5:12 says God performed "many miraculous signs and wonders." We do not know all of what God did or even can do today. If the Corinthian believers had not abused the gift of tongues, we would have had very little Scripture on the subject. We could have even more easily said tongues are not a normative experience for the believer.

My point is that it is very presumptuous for some to say either that God does not heal today or that God wants to heal all today. We must let God be God. We must trust Him to move by His Spirit regularly to perform miracles, or we must receive the grace to accept His sovereignty if difficulties are allowed to continue.

God Does What He Pleases

When it comes to God's sovereignty, the question arises, "Can God do anything He wants to at any time in any place?" The way we answer this question will greatly determine our concept of God's omnipotence. Some believe God's power is limited because when humans sinned they gave Satan the legal right or authority over the earth and its inhabitants. This belief portrays a God who would like to do something on behalf of humanity but cannot unless He is asked to intervene. If the believer does not give God access to act, Satan has the authority to do as he wills. This concept causes a believer to be heavily motivated to pray, but is it biblical? There are numerous scriptures that reveal God's power is limitless, unbounded, unhindered. We never see God held at bay by Satan. The book of Job clearly shows us that Satan could not do anything without asking God's permission. David said in Psalm 115:3 that God does whatever He pleases. Paul, under the inspiration of the Spirit, exposes us to a God who operates as He wishes in Romans 9:11-23. One verse from this passage—a quote from Exodus 33:19—says of God, "I will have mercy on whom I have mercy and I will have compassion on whom I have compassion." God's intervention does not, therefore, depend on man's effort, but on God's mercy.

Human beings have always struggled with wanting to "know it all," to "be like God." Satan tried to use this trait to thwart God's plan in the garden. It worked. People have regularly struggled with God by saying, "It's not fair," "God wouldn't allow this to happen," etc. Again we go back to Romans 9:20-21: "But who are you, O man, to talk back to God? Shall what is formed say to him who formed it, 'Why did you make me like this?' Does not the potter have the right to make out of the same lump of clay some pottery for noble purposes and some for common use?" God has ultimate sovereign authority and power. He does not have to be continually questioned. As the believer puts his trust and faith in the Lord, he can rest assured that God will cause "all things to work together for good" in his life. It does not mean "all things" will be good, but that God can and does sovereignly work out His purpose and plan in the life of the person who yields to His authority.

Prayer and God's Sovereignty

Prayer is not to be looked at merely as a tool to bring about good things or to change God's mind if trouble happens. Prayer is a means of communication and worship. It grants the participant communion and communication with God, giving insight, instruction and inspiration regarding His plans. Prayer lets the believer know God's sovereign will more than it informs Him of the will of the believer. Christians must rest in the sovereignty of God, not blindly, like "*que sera, sera*; whatever will be, will be," but realizing that God cares about us. His plan and purpose does not always mean perfect health, divine healing or wealth. Ultimately, we will all experience perfection. Yet, in this world God reserves the right to move as He wishes and to allow different circumstances for each. Granted, Satan tries to prevent believers from resting in God's sovereignty. Sin, unbelief and doubt can hinder God from doing everything He would like to do. Yet, the bottom line is that God is almighty. He must have the right to do some things that seem unfair to human reasoning. He sees things much differently than we do. He has secrets beyond our finite comprehension. The true purpose of prayer is not to impose our will upon God, but to request God to perform His will upon us and our circumstances. "Your kingdom come, Your will be done" (Matt. 6:10).

Satan's Power Is Limited

The Bible clearly reveals that God is ruler over Satan and all his evil spirits. Some believe that healing, prosperity and blessing belong to all Christians as their spiritual birthright. They say that Christians do not experience them because Satan has robbed them of

God Is in Charge

what is rightfully theirs. The only way to receive these blessings, then, is to conduct spiritual warfare over Satan and his demons. Is this really what the Bible teaches? Let's look at a few concepts. Jesus said that Satan has come to steal, kill and destroy (John 10:10). Truly, Satan is a wicked and evil agent who is constantly trying to throw a monkey wrench in the work of God. But does Satan have the power to keep healing or prosperity from a child of God if God wants to do something in a believer's life? I do not believe so.

The idea that Satan has been given a legal right over this world is contrary to Scripture. Satan's power is limited and depends on the boundaries God has set. The Gospels show that when Jesus walked on this earth, He could heal and cast out demons at will. Satan desired to sift Peter as wheat, but Jesus thwarted that plan (Luke 22:31–32).

God uses Satan as a tool for testing, tempting and trying human beings. Read Job, chapters 1 and 2. God's sovereignty is indisputable. God can do whatever He wishes.

Satan's Boundaries

Granted, the Bible teaches that Satan is a wicked being who, along with other fallen angels, called demons, is bent on hindering the advancement of the kingdom of God.

Paul was tormented by Satan (2 Cor. 12:7–11). He was hindered from going to certain places by Satan (1 Thess. 2:18). He had to rebuke demons out of people (Acts 16:16–18).

But on the whole, we see a confident Paul who was usually aware of Satan's tricks and regularly held him at bay. In 2 Corinthians 2:11 Paul says of Satan, "We are not unaware of his schemes." Nowhere do we find that Paul or other New Testament writers claim that Satan kept a miracle from happening to a believer, causing him to fight the evil one for his rightful blessing.

We more often see a powerful God who can cause supernatural things to happen for His children as they trust in Him and His sovereign plan for their lives.

I firmly believe that if God wants something done for a child of His, He will make sure it gets accomplished. God will do anything it takes to bless His children with whatever He has planned for them.

To claim that God is unable to intervene in the life of believers unless they meet some criteria of praying a special prayer, claiming a specific Bible verse or speaking a positive confession, is theologically incorrect. This view places the responsibility for a miracle upon the believer rather than on God.

Satan can tempt, test and try a believer. A Christian should always be on guard against the devil. But as we see from his attack on Job, Satan had to ask God permission to work his evil (Job 1:6-12). God, who was willing to allow Job to suffer extreme pain and anguish, had an ultimate purpose with a future blessing in mind for him. Yes, God can and does allow suffering, but He is always in control and sets the boundaries.

Clearly, the Bible teaches that God is greater and has much more power than the devil. If God desires to heal, bless or protect one of His children, He can override the power of Satan and grant a blessing to one in need. We must regularly be reminded that God is the healer and performer of the miraculous. Humanity has no power in itself. God's omnipotence must be given preeminence in all of our doctrine, beliefs and interpretations of Scripture. When the believer is told to conduct spiritual warfare and wrestle against the powers of darkness, he is being told to resist the lies, tauntings, fears and temptations of the devil. The only power Satan has over a believer is a lie. Satan is a liar and the father of lies (John 8:44).

2 Corinthians 10:3-5 tells the believer to resist anything from Satan that exalts itself against the knowledge of God. God delegates the blessings; the believer resists lies and temptations. Too many believers get caught up in fighting for a blessing instead of seeking to overcome obstacles to knowing God. Spiritual warfare is conducted not so much for the believer to receive healings, blessings and deliverances as much as it is for the advancement of the gospel of Christ, so more souls can be saved. Ephesians 6:10-18 tells the believer to stand against the schemes of the devil. Verses 19 and 20 reveal that the purpose of spiritual warfare is so that the gospel may be boldly proclaimed.

There is a natural friction among the sovereignty of God, the rule of Satan and the free will of man. The question arises, "If God is sovereign over all, does He predestine everything that happens in life?" This is a very complicated question, and the answer is not as easy as 1, 2, 3. Yet the Bible does give us insight into this topic. We must begin with the recognition that God's sovereignty and ultimate authority cannot be questioned. God is almighty. He has the right and power to do whatever He wants to.

God's Sovereignty Defined

To help us arrive at some answers, let me quote from *Lectures in Systematic Theology* by Henry C. Thiessen.

God, as creator of all things visible and invisible, and the owner of all, has an absolute right to rule over all (Matthew 20:15; Romans 9:20f.), and He exercises this authority in the universe (Ephesians 1:11). Hodge writes: "If God be a Spirit, and therefore a person, infinite, eternal, and immutable in his being and perfections, the Creator and Preserver of the universe, He is of right its absolute sovereign.... This sovereignty of God is the ground of peace and confidence to all his people. They rejoice that the Lord God omnipotent reigneth; that neither necessity, nor chance, nor the folly of man, nor the malice of Satan controls the sequence of events and all their issues." The Scriptures abundantly teach that God is sovereign in the universe: "Indeed everything that is in the heavens and the earth; Thine is the dominion, O Lord" (I Chronicles 29:11); "But our God is in the heavens; He does whatever He pleases" (Psalms 115:3); "Woe to the one who quarrels with his Maker—an earthenware vessel among the vessels of the earth! Will the clay say to the potter, 'What are you doing?' Or the things you are making say, 'He has no hands'?" (Isaiah 45:9); "Behold, all souls are Mine; the soul of the father as well as the soul of the son is Mine. The soul who sins will die" (Ezekiel 18:4); "All the inhabitants of the earth are accounted as nothing, but He does according to His will in the host of heaven and among the inhabitants of earth; and no one can ward off His hand or say to Him, 'What hast Thou done?' (Dan. 4:35); and "Is it not lawful for me to do what I wish with what is my own?" (Matt. 20:15; cf. Rom. 9:14–21; 11:36; Eph. 1:11; I Tim. 6:15f.; Rev. 4:11). God's sovereignty involves preservation and providence.[2]

By preservation we mean that God sovereignly, by a continuous agency, maintains in existence all the things which he has made, together with all their properties and powers. This definition implies that preservation is to be distinguished from the act of creation, for only that which is already in existence can be preserved; that the objective creation is not self-existent and self-sustaining; and that preservation is not merely a refraining from destroying that which has been created, but a continuous agency of God by means of which He maintains in existence that which He has created.[3]

The Christian view affirms that God has not merely created the universe, together with all its properties and powers, and that He is preserving all that He has created, but that as a holy, benevolent, wise, and omnipotent being, He also exercises sovereign control over it. This sovereign control is called providence.[4]

As has been said, God sometimes allows man to do as he pleases; that is, He puts no restraints in the way of man's carrying out his wicked desires. Also, God sometimes keeps a man from doing what, in his freedom, he would otherwise do. He uses circumstances, the influence of friends, and inner restraints to accomplish this purpose. Sometimes He controls sin by allowing it to go so far and no further. Finally, God always overrules what man does in order to accomplish his own ends. He makes even the wrath of man to praise him.[5]

Some hold that prayer can have no real effect upon God, since he has already decreed just what he will do in every instance. But that is an extreme position. "'You do not have, because you do not ask'" (James 4:2) must not be ignored. God does some things only in answer to prayer; He does some other things without anyone's praying; and He does some things contrary to the prayers made. In His omniscience He has taken all these things into account, and in His providence He sovereignly works them out in accordance with His own purpose and plan. If we do not pray for the things that we might get by prayer, we do not get them. If He wants some things done for which no one prays, He will do them without anyone's praying. If we pray for things contrary to His will, He refuses to grant them. Thus, there is a perfect harmony between His purpose and providence, and man's freedom.[6]

Any belief system that does not acknowledge the truths quoted above will always lead to unscriptural conclusions. God allows Satan and man certain boundaries under which to operate, but He always reserves the authority to accomplish His will and purpose. Let me quote again from Thiessen.

> There are indications of Satan's work in the various names given to him, for each name expresses a quality of character, or a method of operation, or both. As Satan, he opposes;

as the devil, he slanders and accuses; and as the tempter, he seeks to lure men to commit sin. In addition, the Scriptures reveal the nature of his work directly. Generally speaking, Satan's object is to assume the place of God. Although the Scriptures give no authority for the view that hell is a kingdom in which he rules, the Word of God does represent him as having power, a throne, and great authority (Matt. 4:8f.; Rev. 13:2). In order to achieve his avowed purpose, he sought to kill the child Jesus (Matt. 2:16; Rev. 12:4), and then when that effort failed, to induce him to worship him (Luke 4:6f.). Had Christ failed, Satan would have achieved the first part of his purpose to establish his rule in the earth. Satan employs various methods for the realization of his purpose. Since he cannot attack God directly, he attacks God's master-creation, man. The Scriptures mention the following methods used by Satan: lying (John 8:44; 2 Cor. 11:3), tempting (Matt. 4:1), robbing (Matt. 13:19), harassing (2 Cor. 12:7), hindering (1 Thess. 2:18), sifting (Luke 22:31), imitating (Matt. 13:25; 2 Cor. 11:14f.), accusing (Rev. 12:10), smiting with disease (Luke 13:16; cf. 1 Cor. 5:5), possessing (John 13:27), and killing and devouring (John 8:44; 1 Peter 5:8). The believer must not let Satan gain an advantage over him by remaining ignorant of his schemes (2 Cor. 2:11), but should be sober and alert and resist him (Eph. 4:27; James 4:7; 1 Peter 5:8f.). He should not speak lightly of him (Jude 8f.; cf. 2 Peter 2:10), but put on the whole armor of God and take his stand against him (Eph. 6:11). Christ did conquer Satan at the cross (Heb. 2:14), and the believer must live by faith in light of that victory. As Pentecost states, "By His death and resurrection Jesus passed sentence upon the adversary of God."[7]

We can take comfort in the truth that God is in control. We might not understand everything that is happening in our world or in our circumstances, but *'til healing comes* we can rest in the truth that God is sovereign.

Chapter II

GOD'S WILL AND HEALING

Is it God's will that all be healed in this life?

I feel that the answer lies somewhere in between a "yes" and a "no." Yes, God wants all of His children to be healed, but, no, not all will receive healing in this present life. You see, the Bible teaches it is God's will that all of His children receive His full blessings of salvation. But just when and how they are received is left entirely up to Him.

Evangelical Christians agree that in heaven every believer will be in a state of perfection. No more sickness, death, misery or pain (Rev. 21:4). But some teach that it is not God's will that a child of God has to wait until he gets to heaven to experience it all. They teach that in Jesus Christ we can have it all in the here and now.[1] They assume that if any believer has the right kind of faith and understanding, if he knows how to wage spiritual warfare against the devil, he can release for himself anything he needs: health, wealth, material blessings and so on.

Heaven on Earth?

All of this looks so good. It makes the Christian life look exciting. But does God promise heaven on earth here and now? Does God promise to raise up a superhuman class of Christians that never get sick, have tremendous wealth and resources, and live in luxury? I do not believe so. You can take numerous scriptures, twist them into many different interpretations and make God's will become anything you want. Second Timothy 4:3–4 says "For the time will come when men will not put up with sound doctrine. Instead, to suit their own desires, they will gather around them a great number of teachers to say what their itching ears want to hear. They will turn their ears away from the truth..." But God will not allow man to dictate to Him.

Some say, "If God said it in His Word, it's yours." The problem with this kind of teaching is that it does not start with a sound basis for accurate Bible interpretation. In Scripture, God dealt with many individuals and groups in many different ways during a specific time for a specific purpose. Let me give you an example.

Jesus fed five thousand people with two fish and five loaves of bread, as recorded in the Gospels (see Matt. 14:13–21; Mark 6:32–44). Jesus performed this miracle for that time and purpose. You could presume that it is not God's will for you to shop for groceries any longer, that He will multiply the little you have as

He did in the example of Elijah and Elisha and the widow's provision. Because God supernaturally supplied food in an unconventional way in these miracles, you could reason He will do the same for you as well.

A Specific Purpose, Specific Time, Specific Reason

Jesus multiplied food for a specific purpose for a specific time for a specific reason. Scripture can't be pulled out of context and labeled as God's will for you today. You could invite friends over for dinner, be seated at the table, and pick up two fish and five loaves of bread and say, "God, in Your Word You promised if I had enough faith, I could work the works of Jesus, so therefore I believe you to multiply these provisions to feed my guests." Don't be surprised if you and your friends conclude the evening hungry. Or you could approach a collapsed bridge and say, "I need to get across the river. If God opened the Red Sea for Moses, He can open this river for me. I have been given the power and authority of Jesus' name to do whatever I need. River, open up in Jesus' name! As you promised in the Bible to Moses and Israel, it is for me, too." Dare I venture to say that you will eventually need to find another way to your destination?

This same principle holds true for healing. Many say, "Jesus healed everybody in the Gospels. So in the same way He healed them, I say right now in Jesus' name I shall be healed as well. I claim my rightful inheritance as a child of God." But this presumes upon God's will.

In Luke 4 we see Jesus being tempted by the devil. At one juncture He was told to throw Himself down off the highest point of the temple. Satan even quoted Scripture to back up his request. But Jesus answered,

"Elsewhere in Scripture it says, 'Do not put the Lord your God to the test.'" This illustrates my point. You can take one scripture as the devil did and claim it for yourself, but God would have another scripture that could counteract the one you quoted.

All of this is said to make clear that God has a specific will for specific individuals for a specific time and place. You can't clump all of God's people into one basket and say, "This is how it has to be for every single believer." There are people who were miraculously healed in the Bible. Yet there are also numerous people who were not. God holds the right to work out His plan and purpose for each person. For example, Noah's whole family was spared, while Job lost all his children and possessions. Stephen, the deacon in Acts 7, was martyred at an early age. On the other hand, the deacon Philip, in Acts 8, experienced great success in ministry. In Acts 12 James the apostle was beheaded, while Peter was being miraculously set free from prison and execution. In Paul's ministry many people received healing and deliverance, yet Paul himself was not granted his wish to get rid of a thorn in the flesh (2 Cor. 12:7-11).

God Can Treat Individuals Differently

In the Bible, not all of God's children received a healing. Jacob was crippled after he wrestled with the angel of the Lord (Gen. 32). Mephibosheth, Jonathan's son, had a physical deformity (2 Sam. 9). Paul had numerous physical struggles, as did Timothy (Gal. 4:13-16, 6:11; 2 Cor. 12:7-11; 1 Tim. 5:23).

The subject of healing is not an easy one. It covers many situations and circumstances. Yes, God can and does heal. Yes, faith and persistent prayer can allow one to experience a miraculous healing. But after the prayer is made and the faith is exercised, the results must be left in the hands of God.

God has a plan and purpose for each of us. The same Bible that says, "If you remain in me and my words remain in you, ask whatever you wish, and it will be given you" (John 15:7), also says, "This is the confidence we have in approaching God: that if we ask anything *according to his will,* he hears us" (1 John 5:14, italics added). Notice our receiving does not always depend on whatever we wish, but on what God wishes. In 2 Corinthians 12:7–11 Paul could have said, "God, in Jesus' name I command that you take away this thorn in my flesh now. I believe it's done, and I will confess it has happened until the manifestation is experienced." But Paul did not. When God said, no three times, Paul finally got the message and accepted it. God knows what is best for each of His children. He knows why one is ill or physically impaired. He knows why another is miraculously healed. He knows why one is not receiving a healing. He knows what another must do until healing comes.

Peter heard that John might not have to die. It bothered him, and he became jealous. Jesus revealed to Peter that he would die a martyr's death. So Peter was quite upset that John might experience otherwise. Peter asked, "Lord, what about him [John]?" Jesus answered, "If I want him to remain alive until I return, what is that to you? You must follow Me" (see John 21:18–23). Peter was saying, "If it's Your will to bless John with long life and for me to die a martyr's death, it is not fair. Why can't your will for John be so for me?" When Jesus raised Lazarus from the dead, I'm sure there were widows and orphans standing at the gravesite wishing He would have raised their loved ones from the dead. Why did Jesus raise only Lazarus here (John 6:43–44)?

Jesus showed us He has a specific will for specific individuals. Some are healed miraculously. Some receive healing gradually. Some receive grace to bear up under great suffering. Some will receive healing when they get to the next life. God's will is always best.

God's Power in God's Timing for God's Purpose

If you have been physically impaired or chronically ill and have been praying for days, weeks, months or years and have not yet received your healing, do not despair. Do not give up. Do not give in to depression. Rest calmly and peacefully in the arms of a loving God, who knows much more than you do. He sees further down the road than you do. Entrust yourself to Him. Decide to love, serve, trust and believe in Him no matter what. Realize He has something for you to do in spite of your difficulty. God has an uncanny knack of being able to get good out of a bad situation. God can make a blessing out of a burden. Remember you are His. You are on your way to His eternal kingdom.

- Do I believe God heals? Yes.
- Do I pray for healing? Yes.
- Do I believe healing always comes if you *have enough faith, say the right thing—confess the right formula, claim the right Scripture verse? No.*
- Healing is more than positive confession.
- Healing is more than not confessing your illness.
- Healing is more than mental exercises and right thinking.

Healing is God's power in God's timing for God's purpose!

God's Will and Healing

Consider Stephen and Philip

The comparison between two of the first deacons appointed by the church, namely Stephen and Philip, reveals stark contrasts in God's will. God allowed them to experience opposite circumstances. Stephen and Philip were both men of good reputation, "full of the Holy Spirit and wisdom" (Acts 6:3).

Stephen was "full of faith and power" and "did great wonders and signs among the people" (Acts 6:8, NKJV). The Jewish religious council was very upset about the stir that Stephen was causing, so they summoned him to give an account of his activities. Acts 7 is a record of Stephen's defense. It reveals his keen understanding of how God was preparing His children for the arrival of the Messiah, Jesus Christ. He said, "You stiff-necked and uncircumcised in heart and ears! You always resist the Holy Spirit; as your fathers *did*, so *do* you. Which of the prophets did your fathers not persecute? And they killed those who foretold the coming of the Just One, of whom you now have become the betrayers and murderers, 'who have received the law by the direction of angels and have not kept it'" (Acts 7:51-53, NKJV, italics added).

After the religious leaders heard this they were outraged and became extremely hostile. Now Stephen, realizing he was in a most dangerous situation, could have believed God to provide a miraculous way of escape. God could have sent a great light and blinded all the council members, as he did to get Saul's attention in Acts 9:3; He could have sent an angel to rescue Stephen as He did for Peter in Acts 12:7; He could have sent an earthquake as He did for Paul when he was in prison in Acts 16:26. But He did nothing to rescue Stephen supernaturally.

Was it because Stephen didn't have enough faith?

Was it because he had committed a terrible sin? Was it because there was some type of curse on his family? No. God just had a different plan for Stephen than to rescue him from danger, suffering and pain. The Lord did not take him out of the awful situation, but He brought him through it.

Acts 7:55 lets us understand what got Stephen through this wicked attack. He remained "full of the Holy Spirit." The Holy Spirit was there to comfort, encourage, strengthen and guide him. He also saw a vision of Jesus "standing at the right hand of God." Stephen was able to focus his attention in the midst of a life-threatening circumstance.

We don't see Stephen begging Jesus to get him out of the danger, nor do we see him saying, "Jesus, why me? What have I done so wrong to deserve this treatment?" He, with an angel-like glow on his countenance, exhibited courage and Christlikeness as he stood against the evil accusers.

He was led out of the city to be killed. The mad crowd picked up stones and hurled them at him. He was struck repeatedly, suffering broken bones, contusions and internal bleeding. He fell to his knees and asked Jesus to receive his spirit. Then he "cried out with a loud voice, 'Lord do not charge them with this sin'" (Acts 7:60).

Was God's plan for Stephen thwarted by the evil religious leaders? Did Satan triumph over God's servant and gain one up on the Lord? Or was God's will fulfilled in the life of Stephen?

I believe God's will was done here. "In all things God works for the good of those who love him, who have been called according to his purpose" (Rom. 8:28). God can allow difficulties to happen in life that for the moment look bad. But in the future a greater plan and purpose is revealed. You cannot always see what God is doing in the present in order to accomplish something for His glory in the future.

For instance, we see that a Jewish religious leader witnessed this whole episode. His name was Saul. "The witnesses laid their clothes at the feet of a young man named Saul. And Saul was there giving approval to his death" (Acts 7:58, 8:1). Stephen's actions had a profound effect on Saul. Little did anyone know that God was working on Saul and had plans to use him in the future. This seemingly senseless martyrdom of Stephen was laying the groundwork for the conversion of Saul.

In Acts 9 we see the conversion of Saul, who later became the apostle Paul, the one the Lord used to write almost one-half of the New Testament.

Paul was never able to shake the profound impact that Stephen had on his life. Years later he said, "and when the blood of your martyr Stephen was shed, I stood there giving my approval and guarding the clothes of those who were killing him" (Acts 22:20).

Paul also said, "Even though I was once a blasphemer and a persecutor and a violent man, I was shown mercy because I acted in ignorance and unbelief. The grace of our Lord was poured out on me abundantly along with faith and love that are in Christ Jesus. This *is* a trustworthy saying that deserves full acceptance. Christ Jesus came into the world to save sinners—of whom I am the worst. But for that very reason I was shown mercy so that in me, the worst of sinners, Christ Jesus might display his unlimited patience as an example for those who would believe on Him and receive eternal life" (1 Tim. 1:13-16).

God used this incident in Stephen's life to keep Paul humble and ever aware of his own sinfulness. God can bring good out of bad circumstances. The martydom of Stephen also became a catalyst to propel the gospel out beyond the boundaries of Jerusalem to the regions of Judea and Samaria (Acts 8:1).

In fact, the dispersion sent another deacon named Philip to the city of Samaria. In the providence of God, the tragedy of Stephen's untimely death was used to get the gospel out to the masses and begin to open the door for the salvation of the Gentiles.

In Acts 8 we see Philip encounter an experience opposite that of Stephen. Instead of rejection, Philip was received with excitement. In fact, the multitudes with one accord heeded the things spoken by Philip, hearing and seeing the miracles that he did (Acts 8:6).

Is God unfair? Does God play favorites? I think not. God sees things much differently than we do — we judge things by seconds, minutes, hours, days, months and years. But God looks at things from an eternal perspective.

We are stuck in a time frame of seventy years or so. Yet a human life span is nothing compared to eternity. We look for a life of ease, a life of plenty, a life filled with prosperity and blessing, a life where every dream comes true, where all live happily ever after. God does not always grant those wishes.

He allows many divergent circumstances in individuals' lives. Some, like Stephen, go through difficulty, pain and untimely death. Some, like Philip, go through great success and live a long and prosperous life. We see later in Acts that Philip got married and raised a Christian family, with four daughters who were prophetesses (Acts 21:8-9).

No matter what we go through here on earth, we should look forward to heaven and eternal rewards. Both Stephen and Philip are enjoying eternity in the presence of God. Stephen got there a bit before Philip did, but the long and short of it all was that they both got to their eternal destination, where life truly begins.

God's Will and Healing

God Will Get Your Attention

Listen to the apostle Paul's attitude: "For to me to live is Christ and to die is gain. If I am to go on living in the body, this will mean fruitful labor for me. Yet what shall I choose? I do not know! I am torn between the two: I desire to depart and be with Christ, which is better by far" (Phil. 1:21-23).

Paul captures the essence of what I am trying to communicate. He had a proper perspective on life. The success of his life was not measured by how well things were going. He was living for the Lord. His main desire was to follow the Lord regardless of his personal comforts and well-being. If he encountered beatings, persecutions, imprisonments or pains, he remained faithful to the will of God.

In my own life I can relate to this truth. I have been able to see God working out His plan and purpose in mysterious ways. I can see how He used my handicap to get my attention. If I would have been perfectly healthy and physically strong, who knows what might have happened to me? I might never have been brought to the awareness that I needed God in my life.

My handicap has humbled me. It has made me see that I cannot make it on my own. Pain, self-pity, discouragement and disappointment—all have drawn me to look outside myself to the One who can provide me with inner and supernatural strength.

My experience has helped me to see that God can bring good out of terrible circumstances. When I became a born-again Christian at age twenty I was the oldest of nine children. I began to wonder how I could lead my parents and siblings to the Lord. At that time my brother Stephen, with whom I was close, was the only other family member who had come to know the

Lord. How was I going to make my family understand their great need for a personal relationship with Christ?

I would preach to my family, telling them they needed to be born again, read the Bible and pray. But it seemed to fall on deaf ears. I can distinctly recall a time the Spirit impressed on me the importance of just loving my family and sharing Christ's love by my actions and example.

I remember telling my father one evening that I loved him more than I ever had, since Jesus had come into my life. We'd had our spats and disagreements throughout my teen years. I was in the hippie generation and regularly fought with my parents for longer hair, louder music and later curfews to attend either rock concerts or perform at them as a drummer in a band.

Yet here I was now, a changed person. A genuine, Spirit-filled Christian. I know they saw a change in me. Still, no one but my brother and I seemed to want to become more spiritually dedicated.

Jean's Story

After a year or so I felt a desire to attend Bible college. I decided on North Central Bible College in Minneapolis, Minnesota. Upon completing the first semester, I came home for Christmas vacation. During the break, I was asked by my church to be one of three Bible college students to share a brief sermon at the Sunday evening service. My parents agreed to come. It was a big step for them to go to a church of a denomination other than their own. I began to see God working on them.

I went back to school after Christmas break. The next morning I received a phone call from my father. He was crying and very broken up. I could sense something terrible had happened. He said, "Ken, your sister Jeanie is dead." I was stunned. My first thoughts were that I better get home fast. I told Dad I'd get the first available flight back to Chicago.

Jeanie had been out with her boyfriend. His mother had gotten a new muffler installed on the car the day before. Because she had become nauseous while driving the car, she thought something might be wrong, but her son insisted on using the car that night before it was checked out. While the car was parked with the motor running, unknown to Jeanie and her friend, carbon monoxide fumes overcame them.

Someone saw smoke coming from the engine and called for help. When the fire department arrived, they found my seventeen-year-old sister, a senior in high school, dead. Her boyfriend was still alive, and he was rushed to the hospital.

Here I was, ten thousand feet in the air in a jet on my way home. I asked, "Lord, what should I say to my family?" As a Christian and Bible college student I was sure they would ask, "Why did God let this happen?" I asked the Lord for wisdom. I felt the Holy Spirit say, "You do not need to know why this happened. Tell your family to trust in Me, and I will work things out for the good."

I told my family this truth. After much crying and hugging, later that night I got to minister to my mother. She asked me to lead her in the sinner's prayer and to help her accept Jesus Christ as her personal Lord and Savior. She knelt at the table as I had the privilege of leading her in prayer.

I was motivated by the love of God to minister to my parents and family during this time. I decided to skip the January term back at Bible College, which was one class concentrated for four weeks. I ended up staying home that whole month loving and ministering to my family.

The wake was hard on my family. In fact, they scheduled it for only one night because it was too emotionally draining. Hundreds of people visited the funeral home to pay their respects. Many teenagers stood in a line that stretched for blocks outside the funeral home to say good-bye to Jeanie. God gave my whole family strength. We stood alongside the casket so everyone could shake our hands and offer condolences.

That night I knelt at my bed and cried out to God in the deepest, most heart-wrenching cries I'd ever experienced. I asked God to use me to tell other people how great He was and how much they needed Christ in their lives. I saw all the young people and adults come to the funeral, and they all looked so hopeless and lost. I sensed in my heart that Jeanie was in heaven. She had come with me to a Bible study, and I spent a good deal of time sharing with her about Christ. I determined to spend my life ministering the gospel of Jesus Christ to lost and hurting people.

My sister's boyfriend was released from the hospital a number of days after the tragedy. My parents decided to go over to his home to talk with him and his family. It was going to be a very uncomfortable meeting. I'm sure my parents and his were thinking, "If only they hadn't used that car," "If only the muffler had been installed properly." I told my father that it was important that he didn't get angry about the whole thing. At least not outwardly.

I opened with prayer at their home. I asked God to comfort everyone as we shared our grief. Conversation was a strain, and the atmosphere was heavy. But we got through the tough evening.

On the way home we drove by my church, which was in the midst of a "Week of Prayer and Victory." It was a bit late, but the meeting was still going on. My mother saw the cars and asked my father if we could stop in. I wasn't sure if he was too excited about it, but he consented.

When we entered the church, people were at the altar praying. We sat toward the back in silence. Eventually the pastor asked if there were any other people that needed prayer. Out of the blue, my father, who was not a man to share private feelings in public, stood up and thanked the church for their love and support during our time of bereavement. He also thanked them for loving his son, who'd had polio, and said that he'd seen such a change in my life. Then he asked them to pray for him. He walked down to the altar of the church and gave his life to Jesus Christ. My whole family began attending that Pentecostal church regularly. Years later, my father would become a deacon there.

God works in strange and mysterious ways. Jeanie's accident was a tragic misfortune. Yet, it is a divine example of how God can take a tragedy and turn it into a triumph. Out of a terrible situation, He was able to draw a whole family closer to Himself.

Ultimately God is always working behind the scenes, arranging circumstances and situations to get our attention. Everything that happens will not always be pleasant, but knowing that God will work "all things together for our good" (Rom. 8:28) gives us the assurance that His will is best.

A Personal Struggle

In my own study of the Bible and personal experience as a handicapped individual, I've come to realize that healing can come in many ways. Healing is not limited to the physical realm. A healing of soul, mind or heart can be just as great, if not greater, than a physical miracle.

For many years I believed it was God's will to heal all the sick. I preached it as a pastor and believed it as one who needed it. But after years of confusion and consternation, God began to make clear to me a practical teaching on divine healing. If it was actually God's will to heal me miraculously years ago and I didn't receive it—because of lack of faith, satanic oppression, not being in the right place at the right time with the right healing evangelist—my concept of God would be devastated.

For years I played mind games. For example, I'd say, "God has healed me; you just can't see it yet." Or I believed, "God healed me two thousand years ago at Calvary; the manifestation has just not appeared in the here and now, but it will by and by." I became at times a very dejected person, wondering what the problem was. My wife, too, had believed that I was going to be healed. Yet, after many years of marriage, she still had a handicapped husband. Did she continue to love me? Yes. Had she at times been upset and confused about healing? Yes. We were stuck in a framework that said: With enough faith and confession of God's Word, healing will come in His timing. After years of this, we were often discouraged and frustrated, wondering why I was not physically healed by now.

We had to come to the conclusion that we needed a more balanced approach to Scripture on the subject of healing. Yes, God heals. But He also can allow someone not to be healed for a greater purpose. What is important is that the heart of every believer is brought closer to the Lord no matter what the circumstances. In sickness or in health, I will wholeheartedly serve the Lord. We must develop a biblical mindset, one that incorporates all of Scripture into a balanced picture of healing, letting God be free to say "yes" or "no", "now" or "wait".

I do not believe for one moment that when I die and stand before the Lord He will say, "Ken, you did not have to suffer all those years. It was My will to heal you, but you never had enough faith," or "you didn't confess it right" or "pray correctly." I cannot see the God of love playing that cruel game. Prayer, faith and a positive attitude are absolutely necessary in a Christian's life, but they cannot guarantee a miracle. A loving God would not make my healing solely dependent on a certain amount of faith or on saying the right things. But a loving God might have a specific plan for my life, including physical suffering to accomplish a far greater purpose.

No Fountain of Youth

Jesus conquered death on the cross through the atonement. But people will still die and experience the aging process of physical decay. The idea that a believer can store up physical health and power through meditating on, memorizing and applying the Word of God is not scriptural. To believe that a Christian can live so full of faith from the Word of God and the name of Jesus so as to never experience sickness, aging or pain is stretching Scripture. Scripture is not a fountain of youth. One can't store up divine health like a supernatural serum that prevents aging. No believer can ever correctly claim that he will live until he is seventy or eighty, and then just lie down, letting God take him home without having to suffer physical sickness or pain. Psalm 90:10, which says, "The length of our days is seventy years—or eighty, if we have the strength," is not a biblical promise for every believer. It is simply a general statement of a normal life span. Very few of the apostles and early church leaders were able to live to be seventy or eighty years of age. Stephen and James, for example, died young, but they were in the will of God.

God can and does heal the sick. He wants His children to seek Him with their whole hearts. He desires that they endeavor to live a life of faith and total surrender to Him. But He does not guarantee that every believer has a right to demand physical healing as part of his new birthright.

Divine healing is available; and the saint, along with the church, should regularly pray for the sick. Exciting things happen when God is moving. But to say that every child of God has a right to confess and demand divine healing, just as he asks for forgiveness of sins and receives it immediately, is a wrong conclusion. The atonement secured many blessings for the believer, but the blessings are delegated in various ways according to God's economy. I will say more about this in the next chapter.

God's Will — Always the Best

Regardless of whatever may come our way in this life—healings, blessings or burdens—the Bible urges believers not to worry about physical or material conditions. To do so leads us into a temporal mindset. Scripture encourages believers to look beyond conditions of this life.

Every Christian would love to be physically healthy and materially prosperous and live to a ripe old age. But serving God must go beyond all of this. Blessings are not God's stamp of approval, nor are they a sign of His pleasure with our obedience. His will definitely varies for everyone. He balances concern for our earthly comforts with a desire to teach us to trust Him in either struggles or triumphs.

This life is not fair. God will not make things "fair" until He establishes His new heaven and new earth. Listen to the words of Hebrews 10:32-36: "Remember those earlier days after you had received the light, when you stood your ground in a great contest in the face of suffering. Sometimes you were publicly exposed to insult and persecution; at other times you stood side by side with those who were so treated. You sympathized with those in prison and joyfully accepted the confiscation of your property, because you knew that you yourselves had better and lasting possessions. So do not throw away your confidence; it will be richly rewarded. You need to persevere so that when you have done the will of God, you will receive what he has promised."

God's will may not always be sweet. It may not always be easy. But it will always be for the best, with ultimate eternal blessings waiting.

No matter what His will may be for my life, *'til healing comes*, I will praise, serve and trust in my Savior, the Lord Jesus Christ.

Chapter III

THE TENSION:
NOW AND NOT YET

The word *atonement* speaks of the substitutionary death of Jesus Christ on the cross of Calvary. It is a theological term that says Jesus took the place of all sinful humanity on the cross when He was crucified.

In Old Testament times the high priest would symbolically place the sins of Israel on an animal, usually a lamb, and then offer it up to God as a sacrifice for them (see Ex. 12; 1 Cor. 5:7; Lev. 6:24-30; Heb. 10:1-4). When the animal's blood was shed, it atoned for their sins. It acted as a covering for sin or appeasement to God on their behalf. Jesus was referred to as the Lamb of God by John the Baptist in John 1:29. In 1 Timothy 2:6 Paul says Jesus "gave Himself a ransom for all." Hebrews 2:9 says Jesus tasted death as

The Tension: Now and Not Yet

a substitute for every human being. He offered Himself up vicariously for all humanity, and His death made it possible for us all to receive salvation. The benefits God offered in salvation were made freely available to anyone who would receive them by faith through grace.

What exactly did the atonement do for mankind? First, it purchased eternal life and forgiveness of sins. First Peter 2:24 states that Jesus "Himself bore our sins in His own body on the tree, that we, having died to sins, might live for righteousness—by whose stripes you were healed" (NKJV). Here we see, in the context of 1 Peter, the issue is a spiritual healing, a healing from sin. Through Christ's atonement a person can receive a healing of his spiritual life that was devastated and destroyed by the effects of sin.

By His Stripes

"By his wounds you have been healed" (1 Pet. 2:24), or as it says in the King James Version, "By whose stripes ye were healed," does not mean literally that if a believer is sick, to receive physical healing, all that he must do is recognize that he was healed on the cross centuries ago. Some use this verse to mean that Jesus healed everyone on the cross, so all one has to do is receive by faith what is already theirs, expecting it to come into existence. But this particular verse does not only speak of physical healing. Rather, it says when Jesus died on the cross He became the complete and final sacrifice for our sins. Hebrews 7:27 says, "He sacrificed for their sins once for all when he offered himself." All that we need to receive full redemption was won by Jesus Christ when He died on the cross. Man's redemption, regeneration, justification, sanctification and glorification were secured "by His stripes." Jesus does not have to be crucified again. So "by His wounds you have been healed." The word *healed* here speaks of "restoring what was broken," "mending what was fractured." Thus, by the crucifixion of Jesus Christ, humanity was put back in a right relationship with God.

What Effects of the Curse Are Lifted?

Yet you can read in the Old Testament book of Isaiah 53:5-6, "But He was wounded for our transgressions, he was bruised for our iniquities, the chastisement of our peace was upon Him and with his stripes we are healed.... And the Lord has laid on Him the iniquity of us all" (NKJV). Verse 4 says, "He has borne our griefs and carried our sorrows," which seems to say that Jesus' death on the cross broke the effects the curse of sin had on humanity because Adam and Eve sinned and fell from grace in the garden. Because of sin, death came into the world in the form of aging, sickness, accidents, murder, anger, hostility, etc.

When Jesus died an atoning death on the cross, He took upon Himself the curse. Through His death He reversed its legal hold on mankind. Galatians 3:13-14 states, "Christ redeemed us from the curse of the law by becoming a curse for us, for it is written: 'Cursed is everyone who is hung on a tree.' He redeemed us in order that the blessing given to Abraham might come to the Gentiles through Christ Jesus, so that by faith we might receive the promise of the Spirit."

What is that curse? It is twofold: Humankind was cut off from the presence of God, and the earthly realm experienced death and decay. The curse also required that salvation had to be earned by following the law. The Old Testament is full of examples where Israel

The Tension: Now and Not Yet

was told to keep the law that was primarily revealed through the books of Moses (Exodus through Deuteronomy). There were many instances of God's blessing faith with grace—Abraham (Gal. 3:11), Rahab (Heb. 11:31) and many others (see Heb. 11)—yet realistically only a few (high priests, prophets, kings) could gain access to blessings of God. The curse prohibited easy access to God.

Israel understood salvation for the most part was exclusive, primarily open to the Jews and those who kept and practiced the law. Now, the Jewish religious leaders took this to the "nth" degree and made hundreds of laws. But until Christ died on the cross, God's full blessing of salvation was not readily accessible to all humankind. When Jesus died, the veil over the Holy of Holies in the temple was split apart, symbolically declaring that God's blessing and forgiveness are now available to all.

What does the blessing of salvation entail? Some say the word *salvation*, or *sodzo* in the Greek New Testament, means God's total blessing on the whole of humanity—spiritually, physically, materially, etc. They feel that through Christ's atonement any believer can receive God's total benefits. All they need to do is ask, have faith and receive. They proclaim a type of heaven on earth. A Christian, they say, has available to him all he needs to overcome all sicknesses, poverty and problems.

Does God promise us a heaven on earth? Does God desire Christians to learn to appropriate the atonement and thus never get sick, never become poor, never be defeated by a devil? The genuine Christian life goes deeper than this.

Some have taken the Scriptures and twisted them to come up with a slick-sounding, appetite-pleasing gospel. The American dream—gospel-style—says "you can have it all." You can have whatever you confess. The sky is the limit if you have the right amount of faith, the right understanding of Scripture and the right perspective on spiritual warfare.

The Now and Not Yet

I like the explanation given by a theologian named George Ladd in his book *A Theology of the New Testament*. He draws parallels among the atonement, the Kingdom of God and the age of salvation. Salvation is both present and eschatological. It gives partial benefits now, which will be experienced in their totality when the kingdom of God is established on earth at the end of the world.[1] There is coming a special age in the kingdom of God when there will be heaven on earth (Luke 20:35).

In this current age, which theologians call the church age, human beings are still prone to aging, sickness, depression and death. Yes, God gives comfort and hope. Yes, He does grant healings and miracles. He desires that His children call out to Him daily, praying that His "kingdom come and His will be done on earth as it is in heaven." But that prayer will not come to full fruition until Jesus comes back to earth to set up His new kingdom.

In the church age it is not theologically correct to expect to receive physical healing and financial blessings in the same way we receive forgiveness of sins and eternal life. Some would like us to believe it is just as easy to receive a miraculous healing as it is to receive God's forgiveness for sins. Healing *is* in the atonement, but not to the same degree as forgiveness of sins.

Ladd has coined a phrase that bears repeating. It is called the "now and the not yet."[2] We have been saved

The Tension: Now and Not Yet

from sin already in Christ, but we will not experience its full blessing until the new kingdom and heaven. We are "now" positionally seated with Christ in heavenly places, but we are experientially "not yet" there. We are already positionally healed and made whole in Christ, but many of us have "not yet" actually experienced it.

In another book by Ladd, *The Gospel of the Kingdom*, he develops this truth in depth. He says,

> Eternal life has to do with the total [person]. It concerns not only my soul but also my body. When we finally inherit the kingdom of God (1 Corinthians 15:50), that which is mortal—our physical, frail body — will be swallowed up in life. Eternal life includes the redemption of our bodies. The inheritance of the kingdom of God means the transformation of these bodies of flesh and blood (1 Corinthians 15:51). All of us, even though we have received the gift of life, are dying. With some, the descent to the grave will be a long, gradual, painful one. With others, it occurs with shocking suddenness. Some will enjoy a large measure of vigour until the very end. But we are all on our way to this grace, for we are dying, mortal creatures.
>
> God has something better for us. There will come a day when that which is mortal shall be swallowed up in life. The backaches, headaches, jangled nerves, arthritis, strained hearts, ulcers, and cancers will be all healed in the influx of life of the age to come. Our doctors, dentists and surgeons will have no more patients. Our hospitals, sanitariums, and institutions will be empty. Eternal life will

mean the salvation, the transformation of the body.[3]

First Corinthians 15:25-26 says, "For He [Jesus] must reign until He has put all His enemies under His feet. The last enemy to be destroyed is death." This shows us that Christ has bound the strongman, Satan, and has plundered his house. Yet Satan is still allowed to have limited access and power (Luke 11:14-22). On the cross, Jesus won the victory over the devil. He disarmed the devil of his power *positionally* in the cross, but *experientially* Satan is not yet brought under total control. But he can be kept at bay through spiritual weapons.

The process of darkness and death is still at work, and will be until the end of the age. Romans 8:22-23 says, "We know that the whole creation has been groaning as in the pains of childbirth right up to the present time. Not only so, but we ourselves, who have the firstfruits of the Spirit, groan inwardly as we wait eagerly for our adoption as sons, the Redemption of our bodies." That total redemption is not going to happen until Christ comes back to earth.

In New Testament Scripture there is a tension between the "already," the "now" and the "not yet."

"Already" in the past at Calvary, Jesus procured everything for the church. Yet, every single blessing He purchased for us as an inheritance is not readily accessible in the "now" just for the asking. All is "not yet" experienced by every believer, even if appropriated by faith. We enjoy the benefits of forgiveness of sin (1 John 1:9), peace of heart and mind (John 14:27; Col. 3:15), joy and other inner spiritual qualities (Gal. 5:22-23). Healing, material prosperity, longevity, protection from all calamity, trial and danger, etc., are appointed by God for each believer as His divine will unfolds for their lives.

The Tension: Now and Not Yet

Blessings — Timed Released

Dr. Charles Farah, in his book *From the Pinnacle of the Temple*, has likened the benefits of the atonement to a timed-release cold capsule.[4] They are available on a limited basis according to God's will. In the end all believers will be freed from all sickness, pain, poverty, disease, fear, depression, demonic oppression, death—those things associated with the first order of things, as Revelations 21:4 puts it. For now, we cannot glibly claim that "in Christ, the second Adam, we have all we need." Just as the grains of the cold capsule work on our symptoms over a twenty four-hour time period, so does God distribute the benefits of His atonement on His own time table.

Notice all the scriptures that allude to our receiving all of the inheritance in the future, the blessings we have "already, but not yet":

Matthew 25:34: "Come you who are blessed by my father, take your inheritance, the Kingdom prepared for you since the creation of the world."

Until the new kingdom, many can receive physical healing and prosperity, but it is not a guarantee to every believer. We may request it by faith, but God determines how we experience it.

We can ask, we can seek, we can knock. We can beseech God on our behalf. Faith, trust, fasting, prayer, praise, Scripture study, spiritual warfare—can help us to receive a physical healing, prosperity or blessing.

Yet, none of these spiritual activities can ensure a miracle. All is not guaranteed until Christ has sat down at the right hand of the Father and destroyed the final enemy, death. Clearly, 1 Corinthians 15:20-28 teaches this: "But Christ has indeed been raised from the dead, the firstfruits of those who have fallen asleep. For since death came through a man, the resurrection of the dead comes also through a man. For as in Adam all die, so in Christ all will be made alive. But each in his own turn: Christ, the firstfruits; then, when He comes, those who belong to Him. Then the end will come, when He hands over the kingdom to God the Father after He has destroyed all dominion, authority and power. For He must reign until He has put all His enemies under His feet. The last enemy to be destroyed is death. For He 'has put everything under His feet.' Now when it says that 'everything' has been put under Him, it is clear that this does not include God Himself, who put everything under Christ. When He has done this, then the Son Himself will be made subject to Him who put everything under Him, so that God may be all in all."

The atonement has purchased every believer's guaranteed healing, which will take place in the future glory when mortals shall put on immortality, when all will receive a resurrected body that will never be sick or diseased. Because of this atonement, healing is also available in degrees to those in this life for whom our Lord wills it.

Romans 8:18-39: "I consider that our present sufferings are not worth comparing with the glory that will be revealed in us. The creation waits in eager expectation for the sons of God to be revealed. For the creation was subjected to frustration, not by its own choice, but by the will of the one who subjected it, in hope that the creation itself will be liberated from its bondage to decay and brought into the glorious freedom of the children of God. We know that the whole creation has been groaning as in the pains of childbirth right up to the present time. Not only so, but we ourselves, who have the firstfruits of the Spirit groan inwardly as we wait eagerly for our adoption as sons, the redemption of our bodies. For in this hope we were saved. But hope that is seen is no hope at all. Who hopes for what he already has? But if we hope for what we do not yet have, we wait for it patiently. In the same way, the Spirit helps us in our weakness. We do not know what we ought to pray, but the Spirit Himself intercedes for us with groans that words cannot express. And He who searches our hearts knows the mind of the Spirit, because the Spirit intercedes for the saints in accordance with God's will. And we know that in all things God works for the good of those who love Him, who have been called according to His purpose. For those God foreknew, He also predestined to be conformed to the likeness of His Son, that He might be the firstborn among many brothers. And those He predestined, He also called; those He called, He also justified; those He justified, He also glorified. What, then, shall we say in response to this? If God is for us, who can be against us? He who did not spare His own Son, but gave Him up for us all — how will He not also, along with Him, graciously give us all things? Who will bring any charge against those whom God has chosen? It is God who justifies. Who is he that condemns? Christ Jesus, who died — more than that, who was raised to life — is at the right hand of God and is also interceding for us. Who shall separate us from the love of Christ? Shall trouble or hardship or persecution or famine or nakedness or danger or sword? As it is written: 'For your sake we face death all day long; we are considered as sheep to be slaughtered.' No, in all these things we are more than conquerors through Him who loved us. For I am convinced that neither death nor life, neither angels nor demons, neither the present nor the future, nor any powers, neither height nor depth, nor anything else in all creation, will be able to separate us from the love of God that is in Christ Jesus our Lord."

This passage says we are more than conquerors; nothing can separate us from the love of God that is in Christ Jesus our Lord—no sickness, trial or attack of Satan. I thank God for this truth.

Second Corinthians 5:5: "Now it is God who has made us for this very purpose and has given us the spirit as a deposit, guaranteeing what is to come."

The word *guarantee* or "down payment" doesn't mean you don't have it all now. As 1 Corinthians 15:25 shows, all of God's enemies are not yet destroyed. That is why there is still sickness, death and decay. The Bible clearly tells us that this age will never be perfect and that any believer is still prone to disease, aging and death. Hebrews 10:12-13 echoes this truth "But the priest [Jesus] had offered for all time one sacrifice for sins, he sat down at the right hand of God, since that time he waits for His enemies to be made His footstool."

If we were intended to get it all now, why does the New Testament speak of the Holy Spirit as a "deposit" or "down payment" of all that is to be given in the future? Ephesians 1:13-14 says, "And you also were included in Christ when you heard the word of truth, the gospel of your salvation. Having believed, you were marked in Him with a seal, the promised Holy Spirit, who is a deposit guaranteeing our inheritance until the redemption of those who are God's possession — to the praise of His glory." Ephesians 1:3-12 tells us we have all spiritual blessings now in Christ, but all material ones will not yet be fully realized until the future glory.

This New Testament truth helps us to interpret all of Scripture correctly. It helps us understand how Paul could still be in the will of God, suffer pain from a thorn in the flesh and yet pray for other individuals, seeing them miraculously healed.

The Tension: Now and Not Yet

I have a very hard time accepting any interpretation that says Paul's thorn in the flesh was something other than physical suffering. It could not have meant antagonizers or persecutors. How could Paul ask God to stop people from persecuting him? He readily understood that "everyone who wants to live a godly life in Christ Jesus will be persecuted" (2 Tim. 3:12). Various scriptures show us Paul did get sick and suffered so much that it became necessary to have a traveling companion, a personal physician named Luke (Gal. 4:13-16; Acts 27:3; Col. 4:14). Scripture also shows that Paul doesn't chide Timothy for his lack of faith for having stomach problems or frequent illnesses (1 Tim. 5:23), and that Paul had to leave his friend Trophimus sick in Miletus, and Epaphroditus near death. Paul understood suffering was part of life. He regularly sought God's help to go through it, if He did not remove it.

To believe it is God's will that you receive and experience all of the material promises in the Bible, especially those of the Old Testament directly relating to Israel, is not correct biblical interpretation. When 2 Corinthians 1:20 says, "For no matter how many promises God has made, they are 'yes' in Christ," it does not mean that a believer can grab any promise in the Bible and claim it as his own. The context of this verse is that in Jesus Christ the promise of salvation to all who believe is certain and finds its "yes" and "amen" in Him. Verse 22 refers again to the theme of a believer "not getting it all" until the end when it says, "He anointed us, set His seal of ownership on us, and put His Spirit in our hearts as a deposit, guaranteeing what is to come." Notice again the Bible teaches the point that, yes, through Christ's atonement on the cross, He purchased everything for lost humanity. But because we are still living in this present world, we will not experience all of the benefits until the life that is to come.

Salvation Complete: Experienced Progressively

Taken out of context, certain scriptures may be intepreted to mean that our sanctification is guaranteed immediately. They can seem to say that we can reach a plane where we no longer commit sin, thus attaining spiritual perfection in this life. But experientially we know this is not true (1 John 2:1, 3:4-6, 3:7-10).

Our sanctification is complete in the sense that we are made holy and set in right standing with God by faith through Calvary. But our process of sanctification is experienced progressively. No one will reach sinless perfection in this life (Phil. 3:12-14, 1 John 1:9-10, 2:1b-2).

It has been said that "sickness and death have come upon the human family because of sin, and that these are not a blessing but a curse permitted by God to fall upon man because of his disobedience."[5]

This is an accurate and theologically sound statement. But the following conclusions based on this statement have confused the truth about divine healing.

Conclusion 1: "Since the devil and sin are the causes of disease and death, and since Jesus Christ defeated Satan and sin on the cross of Calvary, therefore, Satan, sin and sickness can have no part in the life of a child of God."

Conclusion 2: "Since sickness and death are a result of the curse, and since Jesus Christ was made a curse for mankind, one can be set free from any results of the curse."

Conclusion 3: "Through the atonement of Jesus Christ, full provision is made for physical healing, as well as for deliverance from guilt of sin, penalty for sin and the power of sin."

Conclusion 4: "One can receive any benefits from the atonement in this life if appropriated by faith."

Conclusion 5: "It is God's will to heal all the sick, all of the time, in this present life."[6]

These dangerous conclusions come from numerous faith teachers and, in fact, are directly quoted from the late P.C. Nelson, *Bible Doctrines*, pages 97-98. The difficulties with these conclusions are numerous. Granted, the atonement is the basis of every blessing we receive from God, as G. Raymond Carlson teaches in *Our Faith and Fellowship*, a study of the Assemblies of God history and beliefs. But unlike P.C. Nelson, Carlson states that the receiving of all these benefits is partial and progressive. "Forgiveness of sins now is received in conjunction with the redemption of our souls. When we are caught up to meet the Lord in the air, we shall receive the redemption of our bodies and shall be changed into His likeness. Divine healing provides a foretaste of this and comes to us through Christ's atoning work."[7]

Carlson went on to say, "In humility I acknowledge that I don't understand everything about divine healing. Some receive healing but others do not. At times the answer may be obvious, at other times it is not."[8] Why some get healed and others do not can be a mystery. But realistically the answer becomes clear when we understand that in this present life God has a different agenda.

The Atonement Defined

In 1974 the Assemblies of God published a position paper entitled "Divine Healing an Integral Part of the Gospel." In it they address the issue of the atonement of Christ:

Under the Law attention is given to the priests whose ministry points to our great High Priest who is touched with the feeling of our infirmities (Hebrews 4:14,15). The priests, through the sprinkling of the blood of the sacrifices, made atonement for the sins of the people.

An examination of the atonement in the Hebrew Bible shows that in most cases it refers to a ransom price paid for redemption and restoration. This points to the redemption through Christ where He shed His blood in our behalf and in our stead. God has set Him forth to be a propitiation, (literally a mercy seat) through faith in His blood (Romans 3:25).

The reference to the mercy seat goes back to Leviticus 16, where the high priest went once a year to sprinkle the blood of a sin offering on the mercy seat, the solid gold lid placed on the top of the ark of the covenant. In the ark were the tables of stone of the Law which the people had broken.

The broken Law called for judgment and death. But when the blood of a spotless lamb was sprinkled, representing the sinless life of Christ, God saw that sinless life instead of the broken Law and could give mercy and blessing.

"The primary purpose of the atonement was cleansing from sin (Leviticus 16:30, see also Romans 5:11 where 'atonement' is the same word translated 'reconciliation' in Romans 11:15 and 2 Corinthians 5:18,19). It is also clear, however, that atonement brought release from the penalty and consequences of

The Tension: Now and Not Yet

sin in order to bring restoration to God's blessing and favor."[9]

It is taught that in the atonement Jesus Christ paid for the penalty and curse that sin brought upon the earth, and mankind in particular. But it is also clear that all the results of what Christ accomplished through His atonement on Calvary's cross were not brought into fruition in the world.

Jesus, through the atonement, gained mankind redemption from sin and the redemption of our bodies. But the benefits of the redemption from sin are immediate through forgiveness of sins by His blood. The full benefits of the redemption of our bodies are gradual and will not totally be experienced until the end of time."

Yes, the finished work of Christ stands full and complete, but experientially the complete results of that work will not be fully realized until Jesus comes again and establishes His new Kingdom. That is when there will be no more sickness and pain.

The paper goes on, "The Bible indicates, however, that until Jesus comes we groan because we have not yet received the redemption of our bodies (Romans 8:23). Only when the dead in Christ rise and we are changed do we receive our new bodies which are like His glorious body (1 Corinthians 15:42-44, 51-54). No one in the New Testament demanded healing. People came to Jesus beseeching Him. They did not look on healing as their right, but as a gracious privilege extended to them. As the privilege of believers, the promise of healing does not rule out suffering for Christ's sake and the gospels. Neither is divine healing a substitute for obedience to the rules of physical and mental health or a means of avoiding the effects of old age."[10]

It appears that from P.C. Nelson to G. Raymond Carlson to this position paper, the Assemblies of God has struggled to arrive at a more balanced theology of healing in the atonement.

Concept of Firstfruits

The New Testament regularly speaks of a divine delay. We see that not everything will be brought under subjection to Christ or the Christian until the end.

As we have seen, the Holy Spirit is referred to as the down payment, the deposit, the firstfruits guaranteeing what is to come (see Eph. 1:13-14). Yes, the best is yet to come!

George Ladd comments on this by beautifully bringing out the meaning behind the concept of firstfruits. I quote from his book *The Gospel of the Kingdom.*

> In Romans 8:22-23, Paul is describing the future redemption of the whole creation in The Age to Come, the day when God's redemptive purpose will be completed and the creation will be delivered from the bondage of corruption into the glorious liberty of the sons of God. "We know that the whole creation has been groaning in travail together until now; and not only the creation, but we ourselves, who have the firstfruits of the Spirit, we groan inwardly as we wait for adoption as sons, the redemption of our bodies." Here we have the same wonderful truth again. Some day our very bodies are to be redeemed. Some day the whole physical creation is to be transformed. Some day the life which flows from Christ's resurrection

The Tension: Now and Not Yet

will renovate the whole structure of human existence. Until that day, what? We groan: we are burdened. We have pain. We suffer. We die. But not only so: we have the firstfruits of the Spirit.

What are firstfruits? Let me illustrate firstfruits by some fruit trees in my garden. In the late winter, I prune the trees and spray them. When spring comes, the blossoms break out and I know the trees are alive. But blossoms are not firstfruits. They are promise, for if there were no blossoms there would certainly be no fruit; but I have seen trees loaded with blossoms which never produced fruit. After the blossoms the leaves break out, but there is as yet no fruit. Soon after the leaves the little hard green fruit sets. Is this the firstfruits? One year, one tree was loaded with small hard plums, but later there came a wind storm which blew them all off of the tree. I had a peck of small green plums on the ground, but I had no harvest. This is not the firstfruits.

Firstfruits come when the fruit has begun to ripen. You watch the tree day by day. Then comes the day when that first peach is at last ripe. You have been waiting for that day and you pick off that luscious peach, the first peach of the season, the only one on the tree which is quite edible. All the rest are a little green, too hard to be eaten. But here is one peach. You sink your teeth into it and the juice titillates your taste buds, and you revel in the flavour of the first peach. That is the firstfruits. It is not the harvest, but it is the beginning of the harvest. It is more than promise; it is experience. It is reality. It is possession.

God has given us His Spirit as the firstfruits of the life to come in the resurrection. When Christ comes, we will receive the harvest—the fulness of life from God's Spirit. But God has already given to us His Spirit as a firstfruits, a foretaste, an initial experience of that future heavenly life.

Has the realization gripped you that the very life of heaven itself dwells within you here and now? Did you ever know that? I am afraid we live most of our life in terms of promise. We often sing of the future, and so we ought to sing. Our Gospel is a Gospel of glorious promise and hope. Yes, the best, the glorious best, is yet to be. And yet we are not to live alone for the future. The future has already begun. The Age to Come has reached into This Age; the Kingdom of God has come unto you. The eternal life which belongs to tomorrow is here today. The fellowship which we shall know when we see Him face to face is already ours, in part but in reality. The transforming life of the Spirit of God which will one day transform our bodies has come to indwell us and to transform our characters and personalities.[11]

Scripture tells us "We do not lose heart. Though inwardly we are wasting away...while we are in this [body] we groan and are burdened, we...wish to be ...clothed with our heavenly [body] so that what is mortal may be swallowed up by life. Now it is God who has made us for this very purpose and He has given us the Spirit as a deposit, guaranteeing what is to come" (2 Cor. 4:16—5:5).

The Tension: Now and Not Yet

God's Word readily acknowledges that the believer is mortal and will experience signs of his mortality—sickness, pains and aging, to name a few. Nowhere in Scripture is a saint told that complete and constant divine health is to be expected. Of course, no believer should become a hypochondriac and look for sickness to be his partner in life. Healing is available, and a Christian should pray for it, along with getting proper rest, nutrition and exercise. But it must be understood that divine health is no guarantee for any believer if they simply have enough faith. The Word of God cannot be used as a serum against sickness and disease.

The believer is not to be so caught up in this life, anyway. If healing and good health come, praise the Lord. But if not, praise the Lord anyway. The Christian should not be tied into the world system of materialism and creature comforts.

Paul summarizes it by saying under the inspiration of the Holy Spirit: "Our citizenship is in heaven. And we eagerly await a Savior from there, the Lord Jesus Christ, who, by the power that enables Him to bring everything under His control, will transform our lowly bodies so that they will be like His glorious body" (Phil.3:20–21).

The New Covenant — a New Heart

Jesus taught that His kingdom is not of this world. Paul taught that the kingdom of God is not meat and drink but righteousness, peace and joy in the Holy Spirit (Rom. 14:7). The New Testament teaches that the covenant God has entered into with the believer is not a material one as in the Old Testament, but is a spiritual one.

Hebrews 8:7–13. "For if there had been nothing wrong with that first covenant, no place would have been sought for another. But God found fault with the people and said: 'The time is coming, declares the Lord, when I will make a new covenant with the house of Israel and with the house of Judah. It will not be like the covenant I made with their forefathers when I took them by the hand to lead them out of Egypt, because they did not remain faithful to my covenant, and I turned away from them, declares the Lord. This is the covenant I will make with the house of Israel after that time,' declares the Lord. 'I will put my laws in their minds and write them on their hearts. I will be their God, and they will be my people. No longer will a man teach his neighbor, or a man his brother, saying, "Know the Lord," because they will all know me, from the least of them to the greatest. For I will forgive their wickedness and will remember their sins no more.' By calling this covenant 'new,' he has made the first one obsolete; and what is obsolete and aging will soon disappear."

The new covenant has to do with the human heart. It means having God's law in our minds and hearts, knowing God personally and living in the forgiveness of sins. It has to do with a new heart, as the Lord promised in Ezekiel.

Ezekiel 36:25-27. "I will sprinkle clean water on you, and you will be clean;...I will give you a new heart and put a new spirit in you; I will remove from you your heart of stone and give you a heart of flesh. And I will put my Spirit in you and move you to follow my decrees and be careful to keep my laws."

The new covenant does not say that God has bound Himself to heal any believer who meets certain requirements. The new covenant is more spiritual in nature. It is more concerned with a believer's heart and spiritual framework as opposed to the material things of life. While the Jews had a covenant for material blessings (Deut. 28)—houses, lands, children, livestock, physical healing, wealth, etc.,—the New Testament covenant is more concerned with the heart of man and spiritual blessings. "Praise be to the God and Father of our Lord Jesus Christ, who has blessed us in the heavenly realm with every spiritual blessing in Christ" (Eph. 1:3).

The First Installment

The atonement purchased for the believer his glorified body, which he will receive at the resurrection, and not before. It purchased eternal life for him, but that doesn't mean we don't have to die a physical death. The atonement purchased sanctification for him, which means he is holy, saved from sin and set apart for God. But this does not mean the believer can expect sinless perfection in this life.

All the blessings of the atonement have been purchased by Christ's death. But they are available and delegated by God progressively. God gives them to the believer in installments. He has set up something like a trust fund. Everything has been deposited in the account, but it is not all available to be taken out at one time.

Certain blessings are in the first installment, such as forgiveness of sins, peace, joy and other spiritual blessings (Gal. 5:22-23; Eph. 1:3). In context, 1 Peter 2:24 is literally speaking of healing from sin. But physical, material and eternal blessings are delegated as God sees fit in His time for His purpose according to His plan. That is why some are physically healed in this life and some are not. Some receive tremendous material blessings in this life, but some do not. Some are spared great trials and suffering, yet others are not.

In the end, all believers will receive permanent

healing, material blessings in abundance, and protection from pain, problems and persecution forever. By the atonement you have been healed. It is not all available now, but it will be.

So entrust yourself unto the Lord. Rest wholly upon Him. Realize that you can trust Him to do what is right as you remain faithful, and determine to serve Him *'til healing comes.*

Chapter IV

UNDERSTANDING PRAYER, FAITH AND MIRACLES

Humanity has always been intrigued about getting answers to prayer from God. This mystery has been pursued by almost every religion. Many philosophies and ideologies have been developed on the subject. In Christianity the question of answered prayer can be very complex. Yet, I believe understanding and practical conclusions can be gleaned from Scripture.

Bordering on Cultic Similarities

My intent here is to zero in on the relationship that prayer and faith have with miracles. Some faith teachers have put together a lock-proof system of Bible interpretation to convince the student that their conclusions are the only right ones. This teaching operates much like that of cults such as Mormonism, Jehovah's Witnesses and Christian Science. A cult's arguments are so tightly drawn that it makes it hard to see any other way of interpretation.

The purpose of this book is not to expound on cults but simply to allude to this twist on faith healing to make you, the reader, aware of the dangers. There are some very interesting books that detail the dangers of this philosophy that has crept into the Pentecostal/charismatic movement. If you are interested in studying more about this, I recommend that you read some of the books noted in the bibliography.[1]

Many sincere Christians have been led astray through the false teachings of those who felt they had a corner on receiving healing from God. There is no specially revealed knowledge needed, nor are there formulas, mental visualizations or positive confessions that unlock the mysteries of the spiritual realm.

Even in the first century much of this type of belief found its way into the church through gnosticism. Gnostics denied the reality of the material world and exalted the spirit realm as the only reality. While the teaching of many so-called faith teachers is not exactly gnosticism or Christian Science, it has at its roots similar conclusions.

When God heals, He heals. It is His miracle produced by His power, not the result of the mind, knowledge or special revelation of the believer. In the New Testament when someone was healed by God, it took place immediately for all to see. When someone was healed, God was praised and glorified. When someone was not healed, God was still trusted, prayer was still offered and hope abounded. But when there was no miracle, it was acknowledged as such. When someone was sick, he was still called sick (see 1 Tim. 5:23; 2 Tim. 4:20; Eph. 2:26–27; Gal. 4:13–14).

To Paul, being healed, killed, persecuted or martyred was not the issue. It made no difference to him. He was going to serve God regardless of the circumstances. Paul had learned the principle of giving God praise in every situation. By doing this he was able to focus his attention on who God is rather than on what He does. First Thessalonians 5:18 says, "Give thanks in all circumstances, for this is God's will for you in Christ Jesus." Hebrews 13:15 states, "Through Jesus, therefore, let us continually offer to God a sacrifice of praise—the fruit of lips that confess his name." Whether a favorable answer to prayer comes or not, the believer is told to give praise to God.

Beware of Focusing on Self

Praise always directs our attention Godward. A teaching that focuses in on your beliefs, your confessions, your rights, your authority or your faith is a self-centered teaching. Paul always directed his thinking to praising the Lord: "Praise be to the God and Father of our Lord Jesus Christ, the Father of compassion and the God of all comfort, who comforts us in all our troubles, so that we can comfort those in any trouble with the comfort we ourselves have received from God. For just as the sufferings of Christ flow over into our lives, so also through Christ our comfort overflows. If we are distressed, it is for your comfort and salvation; if we are comforted, it is for your comfort, which produces in you patient endurance of the same sufferings we suffer. And our hope for you is firm, because we know that just as you share in our sufferings, so also you share in our comfort. We do not want you to be uninformed, brothers, about the hardships we suffered in the province of Asia. We were under great pressure, far beyond our ability to endure, so that we despaired even of life. Indeed, in our hearts we felt the sentence of death. But this happened that we might not rely on ourselves but on God, who raises the dead. He has delivered us from such a deadly peril, and he will deliver us. On him we have set our hope that he will continue to deliver us, as you help us by your prayers. Then many will give thanks on our behalf for the gracious favor granted us in answer to the prayers of many" (2 Cor. 1:3–11).

"Now when I went to Troas to preach the gospel of Christ and found that the Lord had opened a door for me, I still had no peace of mind, because I did not find my brother Titus there. So I said good-by to them and went on to Macedonia. But thanks be to God, who always leads us in triumphal procession in Christ and through us spreads everywhere the fragrance of the knowledge of him" (2 Cor. 2:12–14).

Notice Paul recognized that he could give praise to God no matter what was happening, because God would lead him in triumph regardless.

God wants you to focus upon Him. He desires His children to trust Him no matter what is going on. By praising the Lord, the believer gives Him the opportunity to accomplish His will, in His way, according to His timing and purpose. Therefore, healings and miracles are a direct result of God's intervention. They are not strictly a result of a person's knowledge, beliefs or confessions. They are not ultimately the result of the faith of the one praying or the one prayed for.

I believe God can and does heal. A believer should pray to the Lord and trust Him for healing. When God does not heal, the believer should continue to praise the Lord and serve Him, echoing the words of Jesus,

Understanding Prayer, Faith and Miracles

"Yet not my will but yours be done" (Luke 22:42).

Healings Came Immediately

When people were healed in the Gospels and Acts, they were healed immediately by the power of God. We never see someone told, "You are healed, even if you don't see it; keep believing, keep confessing it and eventually you will experience it." You will never see that in the New Testament. In Scripture, people received their healing right away. All the faith that was needed was a simple trust and openness to believe God would act, and they received it right then and there. Nowhere in Scripture is one told to keep on speaking it into existence until it is there. No one is told, "Your healing is in your mind, your visualization, and your ability to be positive and speak the right things." No, the healing came from God. All the individual had to do was be open to it. Faith is the act of trusting God. Faith is leaning on God and casting yourself on Him for His strength and power.

In the Gospels one blind man didn't immediately receive clear sight at first, but his eyesight became perfect after a few moments. But he did not have to claim or confess it and line up his thinking correctly for days, weeks, months or years until he received it. All the other New Testament miracles were instantaneous, either right away or within moments, as with the ten lepers who were healed as they went on their way from the Lord. Never do we see anything like what is taught today on how to receive healing by some of the major faith healers. Much of what they proclaim resembles Christian Science more than Scripture. Christian Science is a cult that teaches a modern-day gnosticism, denying the physical realm and putting everything in the spiritual realm.

'Til Healing Comes

The Scriptures teach us to pray for healing. When He heals, it is visible to all. It can be verified and documented by a physician. After one prays for healing or is anointed with oil by the elders as in James 5:15, or a believer lays hands on the sick and prays for their healing as in Mark 16:17–18, one must leave the results in the hands of God.

Faith is Trust

The Greek word for faith is *pistis*. *Vine's Expository Dictionary of Biblical Words* defines faith as "primarily, firm persuasion, a conviction based upon hearing. The main elements in faith in its relation to the invisible God, as distinct from faith in man, are especially brought out in the use of this noun and the corresponding verb, *pisteuo*; they are (1) a firm conviction, producing a full acknowledgment of God's revelation or truth; (2) a personal surrender to Him; (3) a conduct inspired by such surrender." *Vine's* goes on to define the Greek work *pistos*, which is called a verbal adjective, translated with the word "faithful." It means "to be trusted and sure." Actively it means to be "trusting, relying."[2]

When Jesus spoke about faith for healing, He was simply asking people if they were open enough to trust Him to perform the miracle for them. Faith is an openness to God, a trust in the Lord, a reliance upon Him. When one asks God for a healing, all he needs is a sincere openness to the Lord that will allow Him to work as He sees fit. Faith is not a tangible item that one can store up like gasoline. Jesus was not saying that healing will come when a person accrues enough faith to tap into God's resources. God's gifts of healing are, for the most part, dispensed freely. Healings are not given out as a reward to the highest bidder (i.e., the one who has memorized the most scriptures on healing, listened to the most Christian tapes or spent the most hours in his prayer closet).

Faith is a dynamic and positive aspect of the Christian life. It is our deep trust in the Lord. It is our belief that God is at work in our lives whether it appears so or not. Living a life of faith does not insulate you from pain or disease. It cannot invalidate death's claim.

Faith—a Positive Force

I have been living by faith now since March 1972. Faith is trusting God, loving Him, believing in Him and relying on Him to supply the grace to do His will. To me, this is genuine faith.

Faith is not being able to write your own ticket, nor is it being able to receive anything you want, or even need. Living by faith does not mean that you will be able to overcome any obstacle, accomplish any great feat or even triumph over everything that comes your way.

Difficulties, trying times, problems and suffering come to Christians who are at various levels of Christian maturity. Christian maturity does not mean that you've come to a place in your Christian life where you can gain a positive answer to every prayer, receive a miraculous healing from every disease, live in divine and perfect health, and stop every bad thing from coming into your life.

A person of biblical faith is able to love and trust God no matter what the circumstances may be. The faithful find the strength to apply the principles of God's Word and hang in there no matter what. Whether a miracle delivers you from your distress, or a supernatural gift of perseverance takes you through your testing, this is living by faith.

I consider myself to be a person of faith. Does that mean I always gain powerful answers to my prayers? No. Does it mean I am able to see multitudes healed and delivered through my ministry? Not really. Does it mean I and others I share with are brought to a place of utter trust in God no matter what is going on? Yes. You better believe it. By faith in God I have been able to take on a full-time calling of God to be a minister, despite a debilitating physical handicap.

By faith I have been able to attend Bible college and graduate at the top of my class. By faith I pursued a master's degree in theological studies. By faith I have been able to establish a wonderful marriage with my wife, Joni, since July 10, 1976. By faith I have been blessed to father four sons: Andy, Patrick, Ryan and Britt. By faith I was given a home missions church to pastor on August 1, 1981, with a handful of people who were meeting in a local school. We were able to purchase five acres, go through two church construction programs and build a strong, vibrant congregation. By faith I have been able to travel as an evangelist, gospel singer and musician.

By faith I have been able to face great physical pain and discomfort from polio, which left me with a deformed right arm, a severe curvature of the spine, the need of a leg brace and various other problems. By faith I have been able to trust and serve God in the midst of many problems and pressures.

God has not healed me miraculously, nor has He spared me from problems and difficulties. But He continues to bring me through life for His glory. I do not believe for one moment that I have missed God's best. I do not believe that God is upset with me because I haven't been healed yet. I do not believe I have a lack of faith or that others around me have failed to believe God for a miraculous healing in my body.

Yes, healings are great and should be prayed for. But the Christian life is more than signs and wonders. The genuine Christian life is being able to love God no matter what and earnestly serve Him whatever the cost may be. I can truly echo the words of the apostle Paul when he said, "Therefore I will boast all the more gladly about my weaknesses, so that Christ's power may rest on me. That is why, for Christ's sake, I delight in weaknesses, in insults, in hardships, in persecutions, in difficulties. For when I am weak, then I am strong" (2 Cor. 12:9–10).

Personally, I could have given up and quit a long time ago. I have had to face numerous uphill battles—emotionally, physically and spiritually. But God has kept me around for a reason. Doctors did not know if I would survive polio, and if I did, how long I would live. They weren't sure I would walk or even be able to carry on a normal life. Yet by the grace of God I've been able to go on, by faith, every step of the way. I continue to pray that the Lord will work in and through my life every day.

Prayer Is Not a Grocery List

The child of God is called to a life of prayer. Many Christians feel that prayer is like bringing God your requests, expecting Him to answer positively, granting each and every one.

Some feel that, with enough faith, you can get the desired answer to any prayer. Let me share a few verses that intimate this: "Whatever you ask for in prayer, believe that you have received it and it will be yours" (Mark 11:24). "And I will do whatever you ask in my name, so that the Son may bring glory to the

Father. You may ask me for anything in my name, and I will do it" (John 14:13–14). These verses could lead one to believe that if you have enough faith, you can ask God for anything. But the Bible must interpret the Bible, as has been stated previously.

First John 5:14–15 states, "This is the confidence that we have in approaching God: that if we ask anything according to his will, he hears us. And if we know that he hears us—whatever we ask—we know that we have what we asked of him."

The subject of prayer gets clouded when we think prayer is getting God to do things for us. I like to look at prayer in a much broader fashion. Prayer is not so much getting hold of God to cause Him to act on our behalf as much as it is God getting hold of us to act on His behalf. Prayer is not mainly to change God but to change us.

Therefore, when we pray for anything, we are saying, "God, I am open to You and Your will. I am praising You and seeking You. I desire to see Your hand and Your will in my concerns. I am imploring You to act on my behalf. I cannot heal myself or perform a miracle on my own. I implore You to intervene on my behalf, according to Your will." Faith is not the measured ingredient that determines the outcome of your prayer. Faith is trust in God to work in your life.

You Can't Ask for Just Anything

B.J. Willhite has written a wonderful book entitled *Why Pray?* He effectively elaborates this point in a number of places. Following are a few quotes from his book:

> God has not promised to be all things to all men. He has not committed Himself to doing

anything and everything we ask. This teaching is right in line with Jesus' words: "Whatever you ask in My name, that I will do, that the Father may be glorified in the Son. If you ask anything in My name, I will do it" (John 14:13–14, NKJV). What a powerful, seemingly all-inclusive verse of Scripture, but the qualifying clause is "ask in My name." I was considering this promise one day while praying, and I recalled various teachings on the passage that I had either heard or read. One brother had said, "It is as though Jesus has given us a blank check on the bank of heaven and has instructed us to fill it out in any amount and present it to be cashed." Well, I had done that and my checks had bounced. Another had said, "Jesus has given us power of attorney; we have the authority to use His name to get what we need." Suddenly I said out loud, "Lord, that does not work. I've asked things in Jesus' name and they have not been done." I had no sooner spoken when the Father said, "Son, you do not know what it means to ask in 'Jesus' name.'" As I thought about that word, I knew He was right. I did not know how to ask in Jesus' name. All I was doing was presenting my "want list" and then saying, "In Jesus' name, amen." It seemed to me that I was using that name without any real understanding of what it meant. The Lord did not give any further explanation, so I got down my interlinear Greek New Testament and *Thayer's Greek-English Lexicon* and searched for understanding. To my surprise, a thorough study revealed that—if expanded to its fullest meaning in English—Jesus was in effect saying, "Whatever you ask by My command and authority, acting in My behalf, for the advancement of My kingdom, I will do, that the Father may be glorified in the Son." To pray in Jesus' name took on a new meaning. Suddenly, the kingdom comes back into focus. Prayer was to be primarily in behalf of His kingdom. I could see it. We have been authorized to act in His behalf for the advancement of His kingdom. When one is deputized by the sheriff of a given county, he is given power (gun) and authority (badge). All deputies know that they have no authority to act in their own behalf. They may not impose their will on others except according to the laws of the county. They must act in behalf of the one who gave them their authority. Our king has given us authority, but not to act in our own behalf. We act in His behalf. We may not use the power given to us to satisfy our selfish desires, not even our needs.[3]

We must have our faith in God—not in anything we do as a religious act. It is presumptuous to think that we will be heard if we pray just right. Faith in "just right" prayer will not accomplish anything. Our faith must rest in a loving God who hears the prayers of His children and knows when and how to answer. He also knows if they should be answered. When we pray a prayer known to be in the will of God, believing it will be answered, it is. Not some of the time—every time. When we pray not knowing God's will, we ask Him to do what He deems best. As we pray with this kind of faith, we know that whatever happens, whatever the outcome, His will has been done. Much of the time our faith in God is not lacking. Rather our problem lies in the fact that we are trying to have faith in ourselves. We mistakenly think we need to pray better prayers to be heard. But faith, if it is to be effective, must rest solely upon the Lord. It must rest in His goodness, not in ours, as I have said before. We must be obedient, but we must not trust in our obedience. We must be righteous, but we cannot trust our righteousness to open heaven to our prayers.[4]

While I'm discussing this matter of faith, let me touch upon the matter of prayer for healing. I cannot tell you why God heals one and does not heal another. To say that it is His will to heal everyone, every time, does not seem to measure up to the way things are. It has been my experience that God, at present, heals some of the people some of the time. I have seen people healed who confessed to having no faith. I have seen people who seemed to have deep faith see no positive response to their prayers. What is the appropriate response to God's promise "I am the LORD who heals you" (Ex. 15:26, NKJV)? What about "By His stripes we are healed" (Isa. 53:5, NKJV)? Receive them; believe them. Pray and receive prayer—for divine healing with faith that God can do what you are asking. And if He does not, He is still God; know that as you pray, what happens is the will of God for your life. We must do what we believe we should, and have the attitude of Esther, who said, "If I perish, I perish" (Esther 4:16, NKJV). I do not always know what is going to happen when I pray. Often I am surprised at the answers, yet I have a made-up mind: I will pray as long as there is life. And, in death as in life, I will say, "Nevertheless, Thy will be done." I hear someone asking, but what about the suffering? Isn't God concerned about pain and death? Does He want His people to suffer? The scripture is clear about God's attitude toward the death of a saint: "Precious in the sight of the LORD is the death of His saints" (Ps. 116:15, NKJV). Though it is not always easy to see the benefits of suffering, we must believe there are some. Paul said he sought the Lord three times about a problem in his flesh. Then the Lord spoke to him and said, "No, I will not take away the thorn, but I am with you, and that is all you need. My power shows up best in weak people" (see 2 Cor. 12:7–10). Paul learned to say, "When I am weak, then I am strong"—the less we have, the more we depend on Him. Greater praise to God comes from those who are delivered out of troubles than from those who are shielded from trouble, trial, or sickness. The mentality of the early church toward trials and persecution can be seen in Acts 5: they were "rejoicing that they were counted worthy to suffer...for His name" (v. 41, NKJV). Paul said in his letter to the Roman Christians, "I consider that the sufferings of this present time are not worthy to be compared with the glory which shall be revealed in us" (8:18, NKJV); he added, "All things work together for good to those who love God" (8:28, NKJV). In the midst of trouble Romans 8:28 is hard to believe, but looking back from the mountaintop of victory, we can understand it. Every turn in the road was important. Every obstacle overcome made us stronger. Each thing built upon another—all were needed—to bring us to the place we are not. Some of us who are older can look down from the top and say, "Come on, you are going to make it," to those who are about to lose heart. We have been where you are. We made it and so can you: "Let us not grow weary while doing good, for in due season we shall reap if we do not lose heart" (Gal. 6:9, NKJV).[5]

Jesus knew who the Father wanted to heal, and those were the ones to whom Jesus gave a miraculous healing. "The Son can do nothing by Himself, He can do only what He sees the Father doing" (John 5:19). According to this verse we see that Jesus claimed He operated under the direct guidance of God the Father.

The gifts of God are delegated as He sees fit. Even the list of all the gifts of the Spirit for ministry to the body of Christ, which are recorded in 1 Corinthians 12:8–10, concludes with a statement that reveals God is in control of the gifts, not man. Healings and miracles are included in this list of spiritual gifts. Verse 6 states that "God works all of them." Verse 11 says, "All these [gifts] are the work of one and the same Spirit, and He gives them to each one, just as He determines."

Scripture clearly tells us that God is the healer. We cannot control God, nor can we dictate to Him what plan we want for our own personal life. "For we know in part...now we see but a poor reflection...now I know in part; then I shall know fully, even as I am fully known" (1 Cor. 13:9,12). Here Paul admits man's imperfect knowledge. There are secrets that belong to the Lord (see Deut. 29:29). Our ways are not God's ways, and His ways are not our ways (see Isa. 55:9).

The Prayer of Faith Does Not Always Produce Great Results

To think one's amount of faith determines whether he or she will receive a healing puts great pressure upon the person needing a miracle. If faith can be accumulated in some way which gains results, the only way you could know whether you had enough faith would be shown if you received a miracle. But one can have a great deal of faith and not receive any miracle at all. In fact, in some instances it takes more faith to love and serve God when no positive answer to prayer comes.

A passage often used to prove that the lack of faith can hinder God from performing a miracle is Mark 6:1–6. This section of Scripture shows Jesus going to His hometown. He probably came to preach at the synagogue He attended as a child and young adult. When He entered, He was met in a mocking fashion: "Where did this man get these things? What's this wisdom that has been given Him, that He even does miracles?" They made light of His miracles. They took offense at Him. Jesus showed sadness that He was not given any honor. "He could not do any miracles there, except lay His hands on a few sick people and heal them. And He was amazed at their lack of faith."

Was Jesus prohibited from exercising His divine power because of their doubt and unbelief? Or was it because these people were not in a place where a miracle would do them any good? The reason Jesus did not perform miracles in His hometown was not because sick people did not have enough faith. We see that in other places Jesus healed people who personally did not have enough faith, like the father who had a demon-possessed son in Mark 9:24. The reason Jesus could do no miracles for the sick in His hometown was because of the mocking attitude of the town leaders. For Jesus to perform many miracles there would be to subject His claims to open shame. He did not need to perform miracles here to cause the town to consider His Messiahship.

Jesus often used miracles to cause people to believe in His claims (see John 10:58). Here in His hometown He knew miracles would not help. When Jesus said He was amazed at their lack of faith, He was referring to their disbelief of who He really was. He was not speaking of their belief in His ability to perform miracles.

If doubt or lack of faith can hinder Jesus from performing miracles, why was He able to still heal some people in His hometown? Jesus could have performed more miracles there but He would not allow Himself to do so because the Scriptures say, "Thou shalt not tempt the Lord thy God" (Luke 4:12, KJV). Jesus used most of His miracles to cause people to repent (see Matt. 11:20–24). But He knew in His hometown, because of the hardness of their hearts, they would not repent.

In Matthew 12:38–39 the Pharisees asked Jesus to perform a sign. Jesus knew their wrong motives and He refused to perform a miracle for them. It is false to think that if one has a lot of faith and belief he can cause God to perform a miracle for him. Just simple openness is necessary to allow God to do what He wants to do.

A Genuine Prayer of Faith

Intensity, tenacity, unrelenting optimism and positive confessions are often equated with great faith. I've been in prayer meetings where this prayer was prayed: "God, in Jesus' name I command You to perform this miracle by the authority You gave me through the name of Jesus; and by virtue of my rights as a child of Yours, I speak to this disease that it would submit to Your power. I loose that power right now and will expect a miracle." The believer, though fervent and sincere, is praying a presumptuous prayer. He assumes he knows exactly what God wants to do in this need and is praying accordingly. The problem with presumptuous prayer is that we do not always know what is going on behind the scenes, and yet we demand that God give us what we want.

There will be times when the Spirit will lead you to fight for a miracle. The Syrophoenician woman in Mark 7:25–30 begged Jesus to drive the demon out of her daughter. Even though He was reluctant, He did so because of her "reply." She wasn't being presumptuous. She knew it wasn't God's will that her daughter be possessed by a demon. She overcame fear, shame and the prejudice of that day to summon up the courage to ask Jesus for a miracle for the daughter she loved so much.

What is a genuine prayer of faith? Jesus, in the late hours of His early life, prayed in submission to the will of the Father. "...If it is possible, may this cup be taken from me. Yet not as I will, but as you will " (Matt. 26:39). He offered His agonized request, trusting His Father to do what was best. That should be our pattern for a true prayer of faith: committing our burdens to the Lord, allowing Him to work out His will and purpose no matter what the result.

Understanding Prayer, Faith and Miracles

Prior to being cast into the fiery furnace, the three Hebrew children prayed: "If we are thrown into the blazing furnace, the God we serve is able to save us from it, and he will rescue us from your hand, O king. But even if he does not, we want you to know, O king, that we will not serve your gods or worship the image of gold you have set up" (Dan. 3:17–18). This prayer of faith allowed God to work His will on their behalf.

How Faith Affects Our Prayers

Hebrews 11:1 says, "Faith is being sure of what we hope for and certain of what we do not see." It is wrong to read into this verse the thought that "faith means if we are sure of what we hope for (healing for instance) and certain it is ours, even if we do not see it, it will happen if we keep on believing." This is not what this verse is saying. If this be true, why do other verses in this passage say something different? Consider verses 13–16: "All these people were still living by faith when they died. They did not receive the things promised; they only saw them and welcomed them from a distance...instead, they were longing for a better country—a heavenly one." Faith here meant these saints loved and trusted God even though they did not receive all they had faith for.

Some think faith means bringing the invisible into the visible realm. They quote verse 3: "By faith we understand that the universe was formed at God's command, so that what is seen was not made out of what was visible." This verse applies to the creation of the universe, not to our obtaining a miracle. God created the world from nothing. We cannot totally comprehend how this happened, but by faith we accept it. Faith helps us to trust in God, seek Him and pray to Him even when we do not understand what is going on.

'Til Healing Comes

Hebrews 11 shows us numerous saints who by faith received tremendous miracles: Abraham and the birth of Isaac, Moses and the parting of the Red Sea, Joshua and the collapse of the walls of Jericho, many who "through faith conquered kingdoms...gained what was promised; who shut the mouths of lions, quenched the fury of the flames, and escaped the edge of the sword; whose weakness was turned to strength; and who became powerful in battle and routed foreign armies. Women received back their dead, raised to life again" (33–35).

This all sounds wonderful, tremendous, exciting, something every Christian wants. We see victory, power and authority. To some Christians, this is exactly what faith is supposed to accomplish. See what all these got by faith. You can, too, if you understand the secret of faith and the believer's authority in Christ. But, wait a minute. The chapter goes on. Through faith "others were tortured and refused to be released, so that they might gain a better resurrection. Some faced jeers and floggings, while still others were chained and put in prison. They were stoned; they were sawed in two; they were put to death by the sword. They went about in sheepskins and goatskins, destitute, persecuted and mistreated....They wandered in deserts and mountains, and in caves and holes in the ground" (Heb. 11:35–38). This last group also lived by faith. They did not receive all the exciting and positive circumstances, yet they were commended for their faith. Did the first group have more faith? Was the second group weaker in faith, thus having to suffer? No, no, no, a thousand times no! Faith did not guarantee a positive outcome. Faith helped the saint experience the outcome God wanted. God opened Sarah's womb; Abraham's faith did not. In fact, Abraham doubted God was even going to do it. He proved that with the episode with Hagar. *Faith means being open to God to let Him do what He wants.* Moses, Joshua, Rahab, Gideon, Samson, David and Samuel were not better people of faith than the ones who experienced bad things allowed by God. The individual's faith did not determine whether the outcome would be positive or negative. The individual's faith allowed God to move and act as He desired and graciously allowed Him to use them in whatever way possible.

The Prayer of Faith Is Not Twisting God's Arm

When we pray, we are simply opening ourselves to allow God to act as He wishes. Praying is not so much twisting God's arm to do something nice for us as much as it is Him filling our arms with what He wants in them. God commended all of those in Hebrews 11 for their faith, the ones who received great miracles and the ones who did not.

You see, faith is not some secret ingredient, some tangible substance that one can accumulate like poker chips that can be cashed in at the end of the game. You cannot measure the level of faith like you measure the level of oil in a car engine. You can't stick a spiritual dipstick down into one's heart to see how much faith they have, assuming if it's full, whatever they pray for will happen.

When Jesus healed people in the Bible, He often said, "Be it done according to your faith." Was Jesus saying, "If you have a lot of faith that I can measure, you will get healed, but if you don't, you won't"? No.

Notice that in every instance when people came to Jesus specifically for the purpose of healing, He healed them. You can't tell me that each of those people had just the right amount of faith. The woman with the issue of blood in Mark 5:25–34 and the Syrophoenician woman of Mark 7:25–30 show a tremendous amount of expectant faith, persistence and openness. Yet the man in Mark 9:23–25 who had an epileptic son from demons had little faith and some unbelief. The blind man in John 9 was healed by Jesus without his even asking to be healed. Jesus healed him because God the Father had allowed him to be blind as an opportunity to display His miraculous work. Matthew 20:29–34 records two blind men who simply asked, "'Lord...have mercy on us...we want our sight.' Jesus had compassion on them and touched their eyes. Immediately they received their sight."

Ten lepers asked Jesus to have pity on them in Luke 17:11–19. Jesus healed all of them with no mention of any amount of faith. In fact, only one of the ten came back to thank Jesus, and He said, "Your faith has made you well." Faith here must mean simply his openness to allow God to work.

The Prayer of Faith Places the Outcome in God's Hand

Praying in faith takes the situation out of your hands and places it in God's hands. Some have said, "Why pray if God is going to do what He wants to anyway." Granted, God is almighty, and He can do things without getting our permission. But on the other hand, He wants to let us take part in His kingdom affairs. Though He could do whatever He wants, often He will not act unless He is asked to. God wants His children to play a part in advancing His kingdom. If God always acted apart from the believer's faith, there would be no opportunities for spiritual growth, discipline or maturity.

Prayer gives the child of God the opportunity to

build a personal relationship with his heavenly Father through communication. If an earthly father did everything for his child without ever being asked, the child would become spoiled and very lazy. It is the believer's job to pray in faith regularly about everything. But prayer in faith does not always guarantee a positive response or the receiving of what was requested. Prayer gives God the opportunity to act in our lives and to work out His purpose in us.

Prayer and the Authority of the Believer

Some believe healing is a right for every child of God, something like a birthright or a special privilege, to be exercised whenever needed. Much like a police officer who has the authority to stop traffic when necessary, it is thought a believer must take authority over sickness and disease, commanding it to leave a person's body. But the authority of a believer is much different.

Jesus gave to His disciples authority to do the works He was doing, but they could only exercise that authority when He wanted them to use it. Some say Jesus gave all believers the same authority He has over sickness and disease to be exercised any time needed. But the authority of God has perimeters around it. It cannot be wielded any time one desires to use it. A police officer cannot operate in any way at any time he sees fit. He must operate on behalf of the city or state that authorizes him. He must operate under all of the laws and boundaries established. So, too, must the believer operate within the Lord's boundaries.

In Luke 10:1–20 when Jesus gave seventy-two disciples authority to perform His works, they could only use it when He told them to. He commissioned them to exercise His authority on that particular mission. They could use His authority only when He gave His command to use it. In Luke 10:1–12 He also told them not to take money or sandals. Jesus was not setting a precedent that whenever one goes out to minister for Him they should go shoeless and without a purse or wallet.

We can only use God's authority over sickness and disease, or even circumstances, when He tells us to. He has not given us a carte blanche.[6] Please remember that God is more concerned about who you are in Him than what you can accomplish for Him. Our Lord wants you to trust in Him with all your heart and to determine to live a life of prayer regardless of the situations, depending on Him *'til healing comes.*

Chapter V

POSITIONING YOURSELF FOR A MIRACLE

As Christians, most of us know that God has a plan for our lives. Yet often our lives are far from wonderful. Many Christians have experienced problems, pains and predicaments. It doesn't take long for a new Christian to begin to ask the question: If God has a wonderful plan for my life, then why are all these bad things happening? This is a valid question, and no one should be rebuked for asking it. We Christians live in a real world. God does not expect us to follow blindly and wish all the bad things away by ignoring or denying them. We serve a God who has entered into our real world. He acts accordingly to senses. When He does something, all can see it. When He heals someone, all can see it, and the one healed is no longer touched by the infirmity.

Not 1, 2, 3 or A, B, C

God is a God of diversity. He has created a diverse universe. Every human being is different, as is every snowflake. Even so, God's healing truth cannot be formulated in a 1, 2 and 3 = A, B and C. God will not be put in a box. What is good for one will not be good for another. What one experiences will not be what God wants another to experience. God might heal one person who has no faith. He might prompt another to hold on tenaciously by faith, standing on the Word until healing comes. Still He might allow another to go through tremendous suffering, and ultimately death, all for His glory. God is God.

Job 11:7. "Can you fathom the mysteries of God?"

Ecclesiastes 3:11. "He has made everything beautiful in its time...yet they cannot fathom what God has done from beginning to end."

Isaiah 40:28. "The LORD is the everlasting God...his understanding no one can fathom."

Romans 9:20–21. "But who are you, O man, to talk back to God? Shall what is formed say to Him who formed it, 'Why did you make me like this?' Does not the potter have the right to make out of the same lump of clay some pottery for noble purposes and some for common use?"

God calls His children to use sound biblical judgment in all things. A believer should not get on the latest bandwagon of new revelation. Healing and miracles have become a big business today. Many searching people are being hurt and confused about God and His Word.

I like a phrase found in Ephesians 6:13, "After you have done everything...stand." I believe God expects us to do everything He has told us to do regarding miracles and answers to prayer. The Bible provides some clear steps a person should take if he needs a miracle. Then the results are up to the Lord.

Second Chronicles 20:15–17 says, "for the battle is not yours, but God's....you will not need to fight in this battle. Position yourselves, stand still and see the salvation of the LORD" (NKJV). I like the phrase that says "position yourself." God wants His children to remain in position to receive His blessings as He sees fit to discharge them. I want to share a number of steps that can be taken.

Step One: Be Secure in Your Salvation

The first step is to secure your salvation. The most important aspect of this life is to prepare to live in the next life. "What good would it be for a man if he gains the whole world yet forfeits his soul" (see Mark 8:36). Coming to the assurance that you are a "born-again" believer in the Lord Jesus Christ is the most important step you can take. When you know for sure that you are a Christian, that you have truly repented of your sins and surrendered yourself to the Lordship of Jesus Christ, you have experienced the greatest miracle. First John 5:13 says, "I write these things to you who believe in the name of the Son of God so that you may know that you have eternal life." First John 1:9 tells us: "If we confess our sins, he is faithful and just and will forgive us our sins and purify us from all unrighteousness."

If you are suffering from a physical illness, emotional turmoil or persecution, it is essential that you know you have committed your life to the Lord no matter what. Negative situations occur in the lives of godly believers, and when they do, it is easy to think, "What have I done wrong? Has God forsaken me? Am I out of His grace?"

Just think of Paul, who was imprisoned almost more than he was free. Saints throughout church history have faced persecution, martyrdom, physical illness and tragedy. Yet they have remained true to God.

You gave your life to the Lord, not for an easier life, but because He is the Savior; you were a sinner, and you needed redemption.

In John 6 we see the miracle of Jesus feeding the five thousand with five loaves of bread and two fish. Many had followed Jesus just to see all the miracles. But Jesus wanted a deeper commitment from the multitudes. His purpose was more than giving out food and healing their bodies. He gladly blessed them with miracles, but He did it more to get their attention so they would listen to the essential message of salvation.

Jesus zeroed in on what He really wanted from the crowd. He said, "I tell you the truth, unless you eat the flesh of the Son of Man and drink His blood, you have no life in you" (John 6:53). He was asking for a total, all-out commitment to Him as Lord, a radical surrendering of their lives to Him. The real issue is genuine discipleship to the Lord Jesus Christ. We must be ready and willing to serve Him no matter what the cost. The Bible says after Jesus made the statement about partaking of His flesh and blood, "many of His disciples turned back and no longer followed him" (John 6:66). "'You do not want to leave me too, do you?' Jesus asked the Twelve. Simon Peter answered him, 'Lord, to whom shall we go? You have the words of eternal life. We believe and know that you are the Holy One of God'" (John 6:67–69).

The apostles realized what Jesus was trying to communicate. They knew that most were following Jesus for the excitement, the miracles, the blessings. Seeing miracles alone will not bring a person to salvation. Jesus wants people to follow Him not for what He can do, but for who He is—the risen King of kings.

Job modeled this truth after he lost everything from his health to his wealth. He proclaimed, "I know that my Redeemer lives, and that in the end he will stand upon the earth. And after my skin has been destroyed, yet in my flesh I will see God" (Job 19:25–26).

"The joy of the LORD is your strength" (Neh. 8:10). True joy comes from knowing the Lord Jesus Christ as your Savior. When you can say, "God, I'm a new creation, my sins are forgiven, and I have eternal life. I am serving You because You are God and the only Savior," then you can handle whatever comes your way. You are in a great position to receive a miracle. You can say, "Lord, I'm in Your hands. I know You can heal me or deliver me, and I ask You to do that. But if it does not take place immediately or in the near future, and if I have to wait until the distant future or even heaven, I'm still going to trust You, serve You and thank You for all You've already done for me."

Step Two: Seek God by Prayer

The next step a Christian must take in order to be in a position for a miracle is to pray. James 5:13 says, "Is any one of you in trouble? He should pray." God tells us to pray no matter what the circumstances. Paul tells us to "rejoice in the Lord always ...Do not be anxious about anything, but in everything by prayer and petition, with thanksgiving, present your requests to God. And the peace of God, which transcends all understanding, will guard your hearts and your minds in Christ Jesus" (Phil. 4:4–7). Prayer asks God to intervene by His power, through His Spirit, in His way, in His time, for His purpose. If I am sick I should pray for God to heal me. I should believe He can, that He will, and expect to receive it. But after I have prayed I must commit the results of that prayer to God. "This is the confidence we have in approaching God: that if we ask anything according to his will he hears us. And if we know that he hears us—whatever we ask—we know that we have what we asked of him" (1 John 5:14–15).

We must approach God confidently. Luke 11:9–10 tells us to keep on asking…"for everyone who asks receives." Now this scripture tells us not to give up praying for our healing. But we don't want to get the idea that if we keep on begging God, we can get whatever we want, like a spoiled child. First Thessalonians 5:17 tells us to pray without ceasing. James tells us, "You do not have, because you do not ask God" (4:2). If the miracle happens, praise God. If it does not come to pass, do not lose heart, but have faith. Luke 18:1–8 teaches that one should always "pray and not give up." Luke tells the story of a widow who kept imploring a judge for justice against her adversary. Finally the judge gave up because of her persistence. Jesus said, "Will not God bring about justice for His chosen ones, who cry out to Him day and night?" Now justice doesn't always mean getting whatever you want. But Jesus said, "Don't be so excited about getting justice. When I return I want to find persistent faith on the earth." So if you are ill or infirm, be persistent. Hang in there; don't give up. Keep on praying to the Lord, and trust Him no matter what.

Step Three: Step Out in the Gifts of the Spirit

Next, a believer should trust God to move among the congregation with the gifts of the Spirit. All the gifts recorded in 1 Corinthians 12:7–10 were expected to remain in operation until the second coming. First Corinthians 1:7–8 says, "Therefore you do not lack any spiritual gift as you eagerly wait for our Lord Jesus to be revealed." He will keep you strong to the end. The gifts alluded to in chapter 12 were designed to help the church until the end.[1] Among these are "gifts of healing" (v. 9). The Holy Spirit will bring gifts of healing to the members of His body. God works all the gifts in all believers. When the body of Christ is gathered together in His name, they should expect the Holy Spirit to move. "All these are the work of one and the same Spirit, and he gives them to each one, just as he determines" (v. 11).

The Spirit desires to manifest gifts, healings and miracles through His body to those in need. The church must remain open to the Spirit, allowing God to move as He desires. James continues in 5:14–15, "Is any one of you sick? He should call the elders of the church to pray over him and anoint him with oil in the name of the Lord. And the prayer offered in faith will make the sick person well." Oil represents the Holy Spirit. By anointing with oil, one is asking for God's Spirit to come upon the sick person and heal him. According to Mark 16:18, believers will "place their hands on sick people and they will get well." God can use a believer as a vessel through whom His power flows. Corporate prayer is also powerful. Remember Jesus said in Matthew 18:19–20, "If two of you on earth agree about anything you ask for, it will be done for you by my Father in heaven. For where two or three come together in my name, there am I with them." It is essential for the person seeking healing to avail himself of the gifts of the Spirit which are always present among a living and vibrant Christian fellowship.

Step Four: Search Your Heart for Sin

A believer should also search his heart, if he is sick or suffering, for any sin that might be in his life. But not all sickness is caused by sin, as we see in Jesus' response in John 9:3: "Neither this man nor his parents sinned...but this happened so the work of God might be displayed in his life."

But some sickness and trials are a direct result of sin.[2] God can use illness to get someone's attention. David said, "Before I was afflicted I went astray, but now I obey your word. It was good for me to be afflicted, so that I might learn your decrees" (Ps. 119:67,71). If a husband is sinning against his wife, his prayers can be hindered (1 Pet. 3:7). First Corinthians 11:27–30 states that before a believer receives communion, he should examine himself to see if he is participating unworthily. Some believers in the church at Corinth were taking communion lightly. They were getting drunk and overindulging themselves, neglecting others (1 Cor. 11:18–22,33,34). Because of their sin some were weak and sick, and a member died prematurely (v. 30). Can that happen today? Yes it can, and does. Serving Christ is a serious matter. Being a member of His body has requirements and expectations. Some sickness may clear up miraculously after confession of sin to the Lord. First John 1:9 says: "If we confess our sins, he is faithful and just and will forgive us our sins and purify us from all unrighteousness." The believer should echo the words of Psalm 139:23–24: "Search me, O God, and know my heart; test me and know my anxious thoughts. See if there is any offensive way in me...."

Step Five: Stand Against Schemes of Satan

Some illnesses and infirmities are directly related to demons. Demons are still at work today. Satan is a liar, a thief, a murderer and a destroyer. He is not going to give up without a fight. Many of the illnesses Jesus healed were directly related to demons. In our modern scientific day, Christians and non-Christians alike think demons are a thing of the past. My dear friend, Satan and demons are real. Paul told us our struggle is not against flesh and blood, but against the rulers, against the authorities, against the powers of this dark world and against the spiritual forces of evil in the heavenly realms (Eph. 6:12–13). If the illness is a direct result of a demon, it can be cast away, and healing will take place. Revelation 12:11 tells us we overcome the devil by "the blood of the Lamb". Luke 10:19 says we have authority to "trample on serpents and scorpions and to overcome all the power of the enemy". A believer must take a stand against the schemes of Satan.[3]

We are told to "put on the armor of God" (Eph. 6:11). We are told to "demolish strongholds" (2 Cor. 10:3–5). We are told to cast out demons. We are told to "resist the devil" (James 4:7). It is right for a believer to pray over someone and take authority over Satan in the name of Jesus Christ. When people are ill or infirm, they should be open to a prayer of deliverance. Yet not all diseases are inflicted by a demon. If every headache was caused by a demon, how could aspirin cast it out? Yet Satan is very tricky and evil. He can attack a believer's body with illness and pain. If he does, the believer has authority over him.

Step Six: Saturate Yourself with God's Word

It is essential for a believer to steep himself in the Word of God. Saints of God throughout the ages who have had to suffer all kinds of pain have come to see the strength that comes from saturating themselves with the Word of God. God's Word is "powerful, sharper than any two-edged sword" (Heb. 4:12, NKJV). His Word can be like an energizing "fire...shut up in [your] bones" (Jer. 20:9). His Word can bring healing, as we see in Psalm 107:20: "He sent forth his word and healed them." Romans 15:4 tells us we can receive encouragement and comfort from the Scriptures, thus giving us hope. His Word is our strength and energy. Ephesians 6:17 tells us to take up "the sword of the Spirit which is the Word of God." Reading, hearing, memorizing, meditating on and studying the word of God can bring healing to us.

Step Seven: Surrender to God's Will

After all is said and done, the Christian must surrender to the will of God and be determined to serve the Lord no matter what happens. Much like in three instances previously stated: (1) Jesus' prayer in the garden— "Yet not my will, but yours be done" (Luke 22:42); (2) Paul's thorn in the flesh—"Three times I pleaded with the Lord to take it away from me. But He said to me, "My grace is sufficient for you, for my power is made perfect in weakness" (2 Cor. 12:8–9); (3) The three Hebrew children facing the fiery furnace— "...the God we serve is able to save us from it, and he will rescue us...But even if he does not...we will not serve your gods or worship the image of gold..." (Dan. 3:17–18).

It is my prayer that this book can help clear up

some of the confusion on the subject of healing. I want to restore hope to those who are sick, infirm, handicapped. I also want to instill hope, love and trust in the Lord, who desires all of His children to live victoriously in Him. So after you take all the right steps to position yourself for a miracle of healing, stand in the Lord, *'til healing comes*.

Chapter VI

SEASONS OF SUFFERING

Let me share some interesting insights I have learned from the life story of Dr. Paul Yonggi Cho, pastor of the world's largest church in Seoul, Korea. The life of brother Cho shows that faith-filled people can be in the will of God and yet have to endure physical suffering and illness. Pastor Cho has been physically ill all his life, beginning with a bad case of measles as a child, to tuberculosis and lung disease as an early teen, to heart problems, fatigue, weakness and stomach problems as an adult.

He believes in healing. He has prayed for many who have been miraculously healed, yet he himself continues to suffer. He does not claim to have weak faith or doubt, nor does he claim that he is not sick when he is. He has learned the importance of trusting God no matter what the circumstances are, and that the most essential thing is his trust in Jesus Christ. God has continually given him strength as he has built himself up in the Word of God.

Not by Bread Alone

Pastor Cho has taught us that some do not receive instant, miraculous healings, but must depend on God totally in the midst of suffering. Through faith in His Word, they can receive strength and hope to go on, until they experience the full glory that awaits them in heaven.

We do not always know what is happening behind the scenes in God's great plan. He is always working on our behalf. Whether for a short season or a long period we are allowed to suffer an illness or physical infirmity, we should always entrust our lives to Him. We should stay nourished on God's Word for strength and stamina, and keep on believing that sometime our miracle will come. That is the real walk of faith—when we trust and believe God even in the midst of trying circumstances.

For those of us like myself or Pastor Cho, who have had to go through long seasons of physical suffering and pain, it is comforting to know God's sustaining power that keeps us going ahead, ministering for Him as we await our healing.

God's Sustaining Power

I do not agree with all of Pastor Cho's conclusions about healing, but I was intrigued by the last chapter in his book *Suffering, Why Me?* In it he says some things that confirm what I believe. He, too, has learned much by his physical suffering. Cho said, "Despite the infirmities and weaknesses which have plagued my life, through the resurrection power of our Lord Jesus Christ I was able to continue my ministry."[1] God doesn't always heal immediately, but He gives sustaining power. Dr. Cho said, "We must discipline ourselves to maintain tenacious trust and confidence in the love of God when our lives are shaken by the winds and storms of suffering."[2] He went on to say, "The Lord healed many, many people as I prayed for them. But I was not healed."[3] "The suffering seemed endless, but it taught me to look to Jesus to lift my faith and trust higher than I had ever lifted them before, to lift them until my faith was higher than my mountains of difficulty. I learned that when I thought I had come to the end of my resources, I could trust even more and lift my faith even higher. This didn't mean my pain and suffering eased. It only meant that I was able to live above despair and continue to walk with God until my healing came."[4]

I like what Cho says here. You see, he prayed for healing, he had faith for healing, he trusted God for healing. Though he had prayed for many who received an immediate healing, he was not being instantly healed. It did not mean he didn't have enough faith for it. Miracles of healing must happen when God wants them to happen.

Cho has believed in God's healing power for a long time, yet he has been sick many times. God has had mercy on him and healed him, at times gradually, at times immediately. Even today he has various physical afflictions, illustrating further that faith cannot dictate the time for receiving the miracle. If Cho had allowed his suffering to cause him to doubt God's ability to work in his life—or even to use him—his ministry wouldn't be as successful as it is today.

Seasons of Suffering

Many Godly Saints Will Suffer

Pastor Cho said, "Suffering served a purpose in my life, making me more sensitive to people's needs around me."[5] He mentions that the Lord spoke to his heart and said, "See, I used you to bless many lives even though you were sick. Despite your weak physical condition, I am still using you."[6]

Like Paul, many godly saints must learn to lean upon God for His sustaining power and strength until healing comes. When you are sick, infirm or suffering various trials, you can feed your soul upon God's Word and depend on His precious Holy Spirit for strength to go on and serve Him, until your answer comes.

Realizing the great truth of God's sustaining strength when personal health and vitality are not attainable, Paul said, "Therefore I will boast all the more gladly about my weaknesses, so that Christ's power may rest on me. That is why, for Christ's sake, I delight in weaknesses [infirmities], in insults, in hardships, in persecutions, in difficulties. For when I am weak [not healed yet], then I am strong [in the Lord]" (2 Cor. 12:9–10). God will supply whatever strength is needed to accomplish His will in your life.

Seek the Blesser, Not the Blessing

Pastor Cho said: "Though everything may look dismal and suffering may become worse, God will ultimately cause all these things to work together for good...if we believe in Jesus Christ, receive the fullness of the Holy Spirit, experience the great love of God, and put our absolute trust in Him no matter what kind of suffering may approach or torment us. We will not be tossed to and fro more than we can bear. If you only seek God's blessing all the time, rather than seeking His will and His kingdom, your egotism will fail when suffering comes to attack you. If you do not have the fullness of the Holy Spirit and you are simply clinging to words of promises from the Bible as your only source of help, your faith will be shaken when suffering comes."[7]

Cho said, "God will ultimately cause all things to work together for good." The word *ultimately* means "in the end," "finally," "farther down the road." This is when every child of God will receive all God has for him. We must seek to know the will of God. If His will is that we must suffer physically for a brief time, or a long, extended time until our healing comes, we will still be strong for Him. A child of God must learn to seek the Healer rather than the healing. God has given me tremendous strength and blessing. He has healed me many times of various ailments. Yet I have a deformity that causes great pain, discomfort and certain limitations.

Pain — God's Megaphone

I would like to end this chapter by sharing an extensive quote from a classic work by C.S. Lewis entitled *The Problem of Pain*. In this excellent book Lewis tackles the complicated questions regarding "Why does a good and powerful God allow suffering?" and "Why do bad things happen to good people?" etc. He discusses human wickedness, man's sinfulness, the results of the fall and why God allows pain in this life and uses it for His purpose.

> God whispers to us in our pleasures, speaks in our conscience, but shouts in our pains: it is His megaphone to rouse a deaf world....No doubt pain as God's megaphone is a terrible instrument; it may lead to final

and unrepented rebellion. But it gives the only opportunity the bad man can have for amendment. It removes the veil; it plants the flag of truth within the fortress of a rebel soul.

If the first and lowest operation of pain shatters the illusion that all is well, the second shatters the illusion that what we have, whether good or bad in itself, is our own and enough for us. Everyone has noticed how hard it is to turn our thoughts to God when everything is going well with us. We "have all we want" is a terrible saying when "all" does not include God. We find God an interruption. As St. Augustine says somewhere, "God wants to give us something but cannot, because our hands are full— there's nowhere for Him to put it." Or as a friend of mine said, "We regard God as an airman regards his parachute; it's there for emergencies, but he hopes he'll never have to use it." Now God, who has made us, knows what we are and that our happiness lies in Him. Yet we will not seek it in Him as long as He leaves us any other resort where it can even plausibly be looked for. While what we call "our own life" remains agreeable we will not surrender it to Him. What then can God do in our interests but make "our own life" less agreeable to us, and take away the plausible sources of false happiness? It is just here, where God's providence seems at first to be the most cruel, that the Divine humility, the stooping down of the Highest, most deserves praise. We are perplexed to see misfortune falling upon decent, inoffensive, worthy people—on capable, hard-working mothers of families or diligent, thrifty little tradespeople, or those who have worked so hard, and so honestly, for their modest stock of happiness and now seem to be entering on the enjoyment of it with the fullest rights.... Let me implore the reader to try to believe, if only for the moment, that God, who made these deserving people, may really be right when He thinks that their modest prosperity and the happiness of their children are not enough to make them blessed — that all this must fall from them in the end, and that if they have not learned to know Him they will be wretched. And therefore He troubles them, warning them in advance of an insufficiency that one day they will have to discover. The life to themselves and their families stands between them and the recognition of their need; He makes that life less sweet to them. I call this Divine humility because it is a poor thing to strike our colours to God when the ship is going down under us; a poor thing to come to Him as a last resort, to offer up "our own" when it is no longer worth keeping. If God were proud He would hardly have us on such terms: but He is not proud, He stoops to conquer, He will have us even though we have shown that we prefer everything else to Him, and come to Him because there is "nothing better" now to be had. The same humility is shown by all those Divine appeals to our fears which trouble high-minded readers of Scripture. It is hardly complimentary to God that we should choose Him as an alternative to hell: yet even this He accepts. The creature's illusion of self-sufficiency must, for the creature's sake, be shattered; and by trouble or fear of trouble on earth, by crude fear of the eternal flames, God shatters it unmindful of His glorious diminution."[8]

This quotation so eloquently penned by C.S. Lewis sums up a practical exploration about why God allows suffering. Though God does not relish or delight in seeing someone suffer, He knows that suffering serves as a continual reminder that this world is not perfect and that the most important thing is to live a life surrendered and dedicated to the Lord and Savior Jesus Christ.

C.S. Lewis goes on to say, "...suffering is not good in itself. What is good in any painful experience is, for the sufferer, his submission to the will of God, and, for the spectators, the compassion aroused and the acts of mercy to which it leads."[9]

Seasons of suffering can and do come into a person's life whether they are a Christian or non-Christian. It is essential for us to see that suffering, no matter how painful or long in its duration, is to convince us that this life is temporal. Let's heed the reminders that push our thoughts toward the eternal things of God.

For whatever reasons, God uses suffering for His divine purposes. In these seasons of suffering may we find our strength and comfort in the Lord *'til healing comes.*

Chapter VII

GOD USES HANDICAPS

When God created Adam and Eve, everything was perfect. They had perfect bodies. They were in perfect health. There was no decay, no potential for heart disease, arthritis or aging. God placed them in the perfect environment, the Garden of Eden. But sin brought decay. Sin brought in the age of corruption. Throughout human history the creation was going to be subject to corruption.

Romans 8:16–23: "The Spirit himself testifies with our spirit that we are God's children. Now if we are children, then we are heirs—heirs of God and co-heirs with Christ, if indeed we share in his sufferings in order that we may also share in his glory. I consider that our present sufferings are not worth comparing with the glory that will be revealed in us. The creation waits in eager expectation for the sons of God to be revealed. For the creation was subjected to frustration, not by its own choice, but by the will of the one who subjected it, in hope that the creation itself will be liberated from its bondage to decay and brought into the glorious freedom of the children of God. We know that the whole creation has been groaning as in the pains of childbirth right up to the present time. Not only so, but we ourselves, who have the firstfruits of the Spirit, groan inwardly as we wait eagerly for our adoption as sons, the redemption of our bodies."

All Effects of Curse Not Broken

Mankind received the judgment to work the ground by the sweat of his brow. Woman was going to have tremendous pain in childbirth (Gen. 3:16–19). This curse of death was going to follow God's creation until the millennial reign of Jesus Christ (Rev. 20:2, 21:4, 22:3). As shown in previous chapters, some believe when Jesus died on the cross, He broke the curse and reversed its effects (Gal. 3:13–14). They believe that anyone who lives in Christ does not have to live under the curse of creation's decay. They think that any believer who applies this principle by faith can live pretty close to the way Adam and Eve lived in the original garden before the fall. They claim for themselves divine health, divine prosperity, and divine power and authority over creation (i.e., animals, weather, environment, etc.). But this perfection is not taught in Scripture. Yes, God can provide divine health for some, such as Moses, who at 120 years of age had 20/20 vision. He can give prosperity to some like Solomon and David, or allow power over creation (as He did through Elijah with the flour and oil, and the rain held back for three years).

'Til Healing Comes

Revelation 21:4 tells us total perfection will not take place until the new heaven and new earth. "He will wipe away every tear from their eyes. There will be no more death or mourning or crying or pain, for the old order of things has passed away." Until then God can still permit and allow someone to experience a physical handicap or discomfort for His glory.

Handicaps in the Bible

Physical perfection is not a sign of God's best and blessing. God gave Jacob a handicap. In Genesis 32:23–32 we see Jacob wrestling with God. He was preparing to meet his brother Esau, whom he hadn't seen since he stole his birthright. The night before they met, Jacob knew he needed to get alone with God. He sent his family on ahead of him and was left "alone." God visited him in the form of an angelic being. Some evangelical theologians call this a "theophany", a pre-incarnate visit of Jesus to earth, prior to the virgin birth. The Lord saw Jacob would not let Him go, so He touched his hip socket so that his hip was wrenched. Finally Jacob let Him go after he was promised a blessing. The Lord gave him the name "Israel," which meant, "you have struggled with God and with men and have overcome." Jacob said, "I saw God face to face, and yet my life was spared." Jacob became physically handicapped by God and walked with a limp as a reminder of his experience with God; "he was limping because of his hip" (Gen. 32:25–31).

God also used Moses, even though in Exodus 4:10 he tells the Lord he can't be His spokesman because of a speech impediment. Does God rebuke him? Does God heal him? No. The Lord's reply was, "Who gave man his mouth? Who makes him deaf or mute? Who gives him sight or makes him blind? Is it not the I,

God Uses Handicaps

LORD? Now go; I will help you speak and will teach you what to say." Moses had good eyesight, yet he struggled with a speech problem.

God allowed Job to be physically handicapped for a season so He could prove to Satan that he was not serving Him because of many blessings. In Job's life we see God allowing another person to be handicapped to accomplish a greater purpose. Paul tells us in 1 Corinthians 1:27, "God chose the foolish things of the world to shame the wise; God chose the weak things of the world to shame the strong." God can use handicaps. God delights in showing His strength and power through human frailty.

Mephibosheth was another person with a physical problem who received God's blessing. He was the son of Jonathan, who was King Saul's son. Jonathan was an intimate friend of King David. After Jonathan died, David cared for his son. He became a type of the redeemed sinner. He belonged to a royal line though he was crippled by a fall (2 Sam. 4:4). He was living in exile from the king but was remembered because of a covenant between his father and David (1 Sam. 20:14–15; 2 Sam. 9:3–4). He was called into the king's presence and exalted because of the merits of Jonathan (2 Sam. 9:5–7). He was given a glorious inheritance even though he was not physically healed (2 Sam. 9:9). During the king's absence he lived a life of self-denial (2 Sam. 19:24). He was subject to persecution and slander (2 Sam. 16:3, 14:27). He rejoiced at the return of his king and cared little for material things (2 Sam. 19:30).[1] As you can see, God used Mephibosheth as a type of those redeemed by Christ. As he was with David, so too the church is with the Lord Jesus Christ. God can use a handicap for a tremendous lesson.

'Til Healing Comes

A Little Understanding and Love

It is time for Christians as a whole to cease fighting with each other about healing, miracles and faith. Jesus wants us to have love and compassion for one another. He does not want us to tear each other down, causing strife, division and hurt.

Imagine how a sick believer feels when he has not received a healing after extended prayer, and a zealous person says, "You did not receive it because you didn't have enough faith."

Is Jesus really up in heaven saying to the suffering saint, "Oh, well, you didn't have enough faith yet to get what I have for you. You'll just have to keep on suffering until you can come to Me with greater faith or find someone with enough faith to pray over you."

This is much like a parent holding up a chocolate bar too high for their little child to reach, saying, "Ha, ha, you can't get this candy bar until you can jump high enough."

Whether one receives a divine healing goes much deeper than one's faith and positive confession of God's Word. Many more issues are at work here, as we have seen: God's purpose and plan, His sovereignty, discipline and correction, the purpose of trials as a proving ground for developing faith and so on.

Believers must become more tolerant and understanding of each other when it comes to faith and miracles. We would all love every believer never to get sick or to receive a healing every time it is needed. But this life is not like that. God is doing more behind the scenes than one can imagine or realize.[2] In 1 Corinthians 13:2 it tells us one can have enough faith to move a mountain, but if he doesn't have love he has nothing.

Trust, hope, faith, love and compassion must be

aimed for by every believer whether infirm or healthy, in good times or bad times. The deeper issue is keeping your eyes on Jesus 'til healing comes.

Exceptions Rather Than the Rule

Sickness, suffering, infirmity and deformity are not God's ideal. They are not God's ultimate will, His perfect will. But when human beings sinned and corruption became a part of this world, they began to experience the sad results of the fall.

Genesis 3 records the corruption. The ground would have weeds and thistles. The atmosphere would be in disarray—arctic cold to extreme heat. Tornadoes, hurricanes and earthquakes would torment the earth. Romans 8:18–22 also alludes to this. When God determined to guide and bless the children of Israel, He did at times supersede the natural laws of the curse. But these times are exceptions rather than the rule.

Some examples: decay of the body—reversed for Sarah to be able to give birth at age ninety; Moses and the Red Sea; manna, quail, long-lasting clothing; even physical healing was available at times in the wilderness; the sun stood still, axes floated on the water; Jonah lived inside a great fish.

Through Jesus in the New Testament we see this pattern of the supernatural continue. The blind saw, lepers were cleansed, the dead were raised, bread and fish were multiplied and storms were ceased.

God chooses to invade this world of sin and corruption at various times in response to certain conditions and to accomplish a variety of purposes. But the fact remains: God performs the miraculous in many mysterious ways. The greater issue with God is not so much making this planet a kinder, gentler place on behalf of Christians. Though at times He does, He is more concerned with producing Christlike character in His children.

Name It and Claim It: Blab It and Grab It

When difficulty comes, the believer must pray and exercise his faith. But Christians should not think that a miracle will happen if they keep on confessing it is theirs, that it is God's will and that eventually they will receive it by practicing "positive confession."

We do not have any instance in a New Testament healing where this concept was taught by Jesus or the disciples. Jesus' miracles, as well as the disciples', were instantaneous. They were on-the-spot divine interventions. The suffering one experienced immediate results that all could see.

We must get back to a correct interpretation of God's Word on the subject of miracles, healing and faith. Let us not call something God's blanket will for everyone if Scripture has not clearly told us to do so. A verse may not mean what it seems to be saying at first glance. The original Greek or Hebrew text must be checked. Various translations must be cross-referenced, and principles of sound biblical interpretation must be applied.

I hope by now you see how easy it is to twist scriptures. Again, here's one that is misquoted often: Third John 2 states "I wish above all things that thou mayest prosper and be in health, even as thy soul prospereth" (KJV). At face value, if one thinks this is God talking to each and every believer, you would come to the assumption that it is God's will for every believer to prosper materially and enjoy divine health. But a further examination shows something quite different. This is John speaking to Gaius, yes, under the inspiration of the Holy Spirit. It is not, however,

God personally speaking to every believer. Another translation says, "Dear friend, I pray that you may enjoy good health and that all may go well with you even as your soul is getting along well" (NIV). A closer look reveals that this was a common greeting used at that time to open a letter. Much like we would say, "Dear Bill, I hope you are feeling well and all is going well for you, as I know your spiritual life is flourishing." This gives you a much different picture of what was really being said. Frequently, passages like this one are interpreted incorrectly. Most of the time it is not done purposely or premeditatively. It is done sincerely and honestly. But the conclusions can be detrimental and misleading.

Inspiration from Suffering Saints

I would like to close this chapter by alluding to a few saints who faced physical limitations but were used and are still being used by the Lord. Fanny Crosby, though blind, wrote thousands of hymns. Charles Spurgeon, a great English preacher in the 1800s, suffered greatly from gout and emotional problems. Joni Eareckson Tada became a quadriplegic as a result of a diving accident. God has used her to be a blessing to millions. She paints with a brush held between her teeth. She sings and lectures all around the world, and ministers nationwide through her books and daily radio program. Ken Medema is a modern-day pianist/singer/songwriter. Though he is blind, he has written numerous songs and blesses multitudes through his music. Dave Roever was literally blown up by a phosphorus grenade while he was in Vietnam. He has an artifical right ear, is missing a few fingers and has numerous places on his body with scar tissue from the explosion. God is using him to be a blessing, especially to young people in high school rallies. Jim Hukill is an evangelist and gospel singer who had muscular dystrophy as a child and uses a wheelchair. He has a ministry that spans the country, and many people have been encouraged by his message. These people, and many others, would love to be miraculously healed. Yet we realize we are in an imperfect world. Things happen beyond our control. God can and does intervene supernaturally. But when He doesn't, His children need to still face life with joy and victory and serve Him faithfully, realizing that, *'til their healing comes*, God can and does use handicaps.

Chapter VIII

SERVING CHRIST: MORE THAN HEALING

I have been a handicapped person for more than forty years. I have been a born-again Christian for more than twenty years. At the time of this book, I've served Christ for half of my life. I say this to share that to me life is more than being physically whole. I have long since worked through having a physical handicap. For the most part, I have not personally struggled with depression or self-pity. I've always made the best out of my life as a victim of polio. Sure there have been very rough times, and there still are. But I have usually been upbeat, fulfilled and successful. I have never felt disabled. I do not even like to label people with the term "physically disabled."

I would like to see people with a handicap do all

they can to make a difference in some way. My motto has been, "If you can still breathe, God can open up something for you to do." It takes determination, perseverance, faith and a burden to serve God and others. A handicap is anything that keeps you from doing what God wants you to do. That is a definite disability. Therefore, if one has a physical challenge, yet is ministering for the Lord, touching others and working in some type of gainful employment or feeling fulfilled in his life regardless, he is whole. Wholeness must start on the inside. While we are still in this world, governed by the curse of the fall, healing must be looked at in a broader sense. Not all sickness, deformity or suffering must be removed or miraculously healed for one to be whole in God. I am in the will of God even though I have a deformity and suffer various physical illnesses. I am happy in Christ, which means in Christ I've already been healed. I am whole.

Wholeness in a Divine Relationship

I am productive, fruitful and fulfilled. My healing comes in my relationship with Christ. My healing took place in Christ when He died on the cross, for "by His stripes I am healed." He has guaranteed me that my body is going to be whole in eternity. Experientially I have not yet received it, but I feel God is allowing me to suffer for His glory and His purpose. Some have said to me, "I don't know why God hasn't healed you yet. He could get more glory, and use you to win more souls if you were healed." But how do they know? That statement is very presumptuous. Sure, I wouldn't mind a miraculous healing. Who with a physical problem wouldn't? But whether I am healed here, instantly, gradually, or in heaven, does not really

Serving Christ: More Than Healing

matter. I am already healed because of my relationship with Christ. The benefits of personal relationship with Jesus Christ far outweigh all the burdens.

The most important thing in my life is not my healing. "To be healed or not to be healed" is not the burning question to me. What matters more is being in the will of God and maintaining a right relationship with Him. I seek the Healer more than the healing. I look at the Blesser more than the blessing. Therefore, in Christ I have more than I need. "I live by faith in the Son of God, who loved me and gave himself for me" (Gal. 2:20). Seeing that I live by faith, I am positioned for an instantaneous miraculous healing any day. But until my healing comes I am already healed because of what Christ has done for me. This might sound like double-talk, but I've been healed from the need to be healed, because in Christ I am already whole. I am in the will of God. I firmly believe that. I have done everything God's Word has told me to do. If God wants to manifest a miracle in my body, He can do it at any time. That might come as a surprise to some who believe it is not God's will that any be sick. Granted, His perfect, original will is not that any be sick or suffer. Eventually His perfect will shall be fully realized in the new heaven and new earth where there will be "no more death or mourning or crying or pain" (Rev. 21:4). I believe until then I must take up the cross and follow Him (see Mark 8:34). "I have learned to be content whatever the circumstances. I know what it is to be in need, and I know what it is to have plenty. I have learned the secret of being content in any and every situation....I can do everything through him who gives me strength" (Phil. 4:11–13).

"[I] know that in all things God works for the good of those who love him, who have been called according to his purpose. In all these things [I am] more than [a conqueror] through him who loved [me]. For I am convinced that neither death nor life, neither angels nor demons, neither the present nor the future, nor any powers, neither height nor depth, [neither a physical handicap], nor anything else in all creation will be able to separate [me] from the love of God that is in Christ Jesus our Lord" (Rom. 8:28, 37–39). "He said to me, 'My grace is sufficient for you, for my power is made perfect in weakness'. Therefore I will boast all the more gladly about my weaknesses, so that Christ's power may rest on me. That is why, for Christ's sake, I delight in weaknesses, in insults, in hardships, in persecutions, in difficulties. For when I am weak, then I am strong" (2 Cor. 12:9–10).

No One Enjoys Suffering

Because of these scriptural truths I have come to realize serving Christ is more than healing. I am open enough to God, by faith, that whatever happens I am complete and whole in Christ. I am victorious and able to stay faithful to Him no matter what. Are there times of difficulties and discouragement? Of course. Do I ever wish that God would heal me miraculously so I wouldn't have to go through the physical problems, pain and inconveniences? Almost daily. I do know God is a healing God. I have personally experienced numerous healings from Him. Still I have a noticeable deformity and chronic ailments. I can't sit around and worry about why I have not received that miraculous healing from the Lord. God has called me to go on each day trusting Him. God does heal. He wants more healings to take place. The miraculous should be a regular part of the life of the church until Jesus comes back.

Through my own personal experience I have been

Serving Christ: More Than Healing

forced to take a practical, theological and workable view on the doctrine of healing. Because of my handicap from polio and my other physical and emotional struggles, I needed to come to some basic conclusions that were not easy to arrive at.

From One Spectrum to Another

I feel like I've gone from one end of the spectrum to the other. I have gone from thinking that God wants to heal everyone if they have enough faith and apply the Word, to thinking He heals very few people today.

According to Scripture and the experience of life itself, there has to be some middle ground—a place where God has the freedom to move by His Spirit and perform the miraculous, but is also allowed to move sovereignly as He wills.

Don't Need the Sensational

Some will say, "Don't upset my beliefs. I am happy believing that it is God's will to heal everyone in this life. It is something that gives me hope. I believe that if I have great faith and confess His Word long enough and stand on it no matter what, eventually I will get what was promised to me in the here and now."

Many people express that unless they live like this they feel no hope in praying. They feel hollow and shallow. Why be a Christian if you can't believe that you "can have whatever you say"? In support of their view they quote Jesus, who said, "If you believe, you will receive whatever you ask for in prayer" (Matt. 21:22).

But one must not be a believer for selfish reasons. A Christian driven by the hope that he can get whatever God's Word says no matter what is serving God for the wrong reasons.

We must serve God because He is God. Apart from Him there is no other means of obtaining eternal life, forgiveness of sins and peace. We must serve God, not for what we can receive in this life, but for what He has promised us forever. We should be driven with such love and appreciation for His mercy that we will be sold out for Him as long as we live.

You see, just because some belief makes you happy or gives you peace doesn't mean it is true. Many people who follow Eastern mysticism or New Age thinking, universalism, Christian Science, Mormonism or the Watch Tower Society (Jehovah's Witnesses) claim to be happy and fulfilled. One cannot take feeling as a standard of truth.

Tried and Tried: It Didn't Work

I tried to believe in the faith theology. I attempted to confess the Word, possess great faith, refuse to confess my symptoms and live by faith in the spiritual realm. I didn't want to have doubt. I did not want to live by fleshly means and hinder the Spirit of God. But after many years of studying God's Word in depth, and receiving truth that matched up with real-life experience, I have had to come to some conclusions.

I have suffered greatly from a physical deformity. I have suffered much pain and frequent headaches. I have experienced digestive and bowel problems. I have numerous physical challenges. I broke my leg twice trying to confess a healing into existence. I do not believe I am suffering because of a curse on me, because I have a demon over me, because I do not have enough faith or because I have not gotten to the right faith healer.

Serving Christ: More Than Healing

I have these "light and momentary troubles [which] are achieving for [me] an eternal glory that far outweighs them all. [Because I] fix [my] eyes not on what is seen, but on what is unseen. For what is seen is temporary, but what is unseen is eternal" (2 Cor. 4:17–18).

As a pastor and evangelist, I have seen godly, loving people suffer tremendously. Even though great prayers of faith were offered, they passed from this life to the next.

Pastor Schmidgall's Story

I was profoundly influenced by a man I worked under as a youth pastor. His name was Ken Schmidgall. He was the pastor of First Assembly of God in Jerseyville, Illinois.

I became his youth pastor in 1979. About six months after I was there, he developed a severe cough and fever that hung on for weeks. Concerned that it might be pneumonia, he went to the doctor. Spots were seen on his lungs through X-rays, so he went for further tests in St. Louis. After tests and exploratory surgery, it was discovered that he had cancer of the lymph nodes. It had spread throughout his body. Ken was only in his early forties, with three children and a growing church.

As a young minister who had experienced my share of suffering, I was always trying to get a handle on healing and faith. I thought Ken's illness surely was not of God, so I trusted he would be healed for the glory of God. We began to pray and seek God. Well-meaning Christians from all over began to build up this pastor's faith.

Ken was a good man, one of the most humble and sincere servants of God I had ever met. He was kindhearted, faithful and totally sold out for Jesus Christ. If there was anyone who was a good candidate to receive a miracle, it was Ken Schmidgall.

He and his wife, Rowena, decided not to go the route of chemotherapy and surgeries. They were going to use prayer, faith, the Word and natural cures like herbs, vitamins, vegetables, juice drinks and Laetrile.

The doctors offered no real cure, just possible prolonging of life. One year went by. Ken was faithful to God, the Word and prayer. He was a blessed example of faith to all who saw him. He and I became very close in those days as we would minister to each other. People would say, "Ken, you're going to be healed, God told me. Just confess the Word of God, stand on all the promises, and you will get your healing."

He did everything possible. Some even told his wife her husband was ill because of sin, Satan or even because of wrong attitudes in the church he was pastoring. But through it all Ken loved the Lord. He said, "It's not how long you live but how you live. I've already outlived the earthly life of Jesus. He was crucified when He was only thirty three." He would tell me, "No matter what happens to a Christian, God wants us to remain loving and faithful to Him."

During the second year of the disease he began to get very weary. He had to stay in bed and use an oxygen tank to help him breathe. He would listen to the Bible on tape and the local Christian radio station all the time. He kept his faith throughout. Eventually he could no longer leave his home at all, but listened to the services at his church through an intercom. After two years of battling, Ken went to be with the Lord. The entire town of Jerseyville watched Ken stay free of bitterness and full of love for his Savior. As a result, many were drawn to God through the life of His

Serving Christ: More Than Healing

faithful servant. Our church grew closer together. And in spite of the physical challenges, Jesus still got all the glory.

A Leading Charismatic Figure

Consider what respected charismatic pastor Jamie Buckingham went through. In the summer of 1991 he released a book entitled *A Summer of Miracles*.[1] In it he chronicled the amazing journey he had gone through after being told he had terminal cancer.

Jamie was a well-traveled speaker and author in charismatic circles. He wrote a book about the healing ministry of Kathryn Kuhlman.[2] He was a firm believer in the healing power of God. Having cancer presented a big challenge to him and his friends.

He went through a long, arduous journey seeking his healing. Well-meaning leaders in the charismatic movement counseled him along the way. He received many calls from those who had "revelations" from God that he would be healed and his life spared. Eventually he submitted to medical surgery, hoping it would arrest the cancer.

In my view, all this pressure to seek healing may have prevented this great charismatic leader from spending time preparing for heaven. It was evident he loved the Lord very much, and the experience with cancer brought him even closer to Him. Yet Jamie went to be with the Lord a number of months after the book was published. I believe at that time he received his ultimate healing.

When this happens, it seems like many in the "word of faith" circles feel gypped out of what was really supposed to happen, namely a miracle of healing. You get the sense that, yes, the believer is in heaven, but he really didn't have to die. Somewhere we failed, someone's faith failed, Satan won a victory. What should be a time of preparation to meet the Lord has been a constant battle of fighting Satan, claiming and confessing healing verses from Scripture, listening to countless people speak health to your diseased organ, commanding it to be restored and so on.

It is fine to do all you can to receive a miracle, but there must come a time when you can rest in the assurance of your salvation and begin to look forward to heaven.

Either/Or: God Gets the Glory

When healing comes, whether through direct divine intervention, surgery, medications or proper diet, rest and exercise, God should get all the glory; for all healing comes from Him. On the other hand, when no healing or miracle takes place after earnest prayers of faith and persistent trust in God's Word, God should still get the glory. A much broader issue is at stake here. It is the issue of love and trust in God whatever the circumstances. So again we get back to the truth that serving, loving and trusting God is more important than healing, or for that matter receiving anything from God. When you have Christ, what more could you ask for? With "Christ in you, the hope of glory" (Col. 1:27), you have all you need. Whatever else comes from His hand of blessing (i.e., riches, healing, miracles or a host of other provisions) is just icing on the cake.

Serve God No Matter What

What is the conclusion? Suffering saints should always have faith for God to heal them. Believers in local churches should always pray and have faith that God will stretch out His hand to heal (see Acts 4:30).

Serving Christ: More Than Healing

Yet the results must be left in the hands of God. The believer—well, healthy, sick, infirm, deformed or struggling—is encouraged by Scripture, having done everything, to stand firm (see Eph. 6:13–14).

We must live by faith, feed on the Word of God and pray believing that God answers. We must wait expectantly on the Lord for His blessing and "not become weary in doing good, for at the proper time we will reap a harvest if we do not give up" (Galatians 6:9). Someone may say, "If I'm not guaranteed that God will heal me, why pray? Why have faith? I might as well just sit back and let God do what He wants." But we never know exactly what God is doing. We do not always see all that is going on behind the scenes. God expects us to be faithful, to be persistent, to seek the Healer more than the healing. Remember the old adage, "Ours is not to reason why, ours is but to do or die." To a certain extent this secular statement rings true for the believer and his God. "Ours is not to reason why, ours is just to trust and try." We must do all we can and let the results remain in God's hand.

I still keep praying and believing God for a miracle to take place in my crippled body. I continue to seek God for divine health. I believe this is what God expects me to do. I will remain faithful to Him. I will serve Him regardless of my circumstances. But I also realize "for now we see but a poor reflection as in a mirror; then we shall see face to face. Now I know in part, but then I shall know fully even as I am fully known" (1 Cor. 13:12).

Our prayer should be, "Lord, stretch forth thy hand to heal [for] our God whom we serve is able to deliver us. 'He will deliver us...but even if he does not' we will still serve him" (see Acts 4:30; Dan. 3:17–18). Let's trust Him *'til healing comes,* because serving Christ is more than receiving healing.

'Til Healing Comes

Chapter IX

THE BEST IS YET TO COME

It is my desire to write an honest book, one not meant to tickle the ears or cause goose bumps and warm fuzzies. I desire to communicate the truth as I've seen through my own eyes and life experience. I am determined to share realistic hope about God and genuine salvation.

Much of what I hear today from charismatic circles is flashy and showy. It has sparkle and glitter. It arouses the excitement in all of us to hear that God wants us to have it all now. God wants us all to be physically and materially well off. We do not have to succumb to sickness and poverty. God desires to shower us with divine health. He wants Christians to have the bigger and the better. He wants churches to have big buildings and large congregations. He wants

His people to be at the top of it all.

That sounds tantalizing. This message will fill the halls, draw in the Christian TV ratings and generate a financial response. But is this the real gospel of Jesus Christ? Is God that determined to make you physically well and financially blessed? Oh, I believe God can and does heal and materially bless, but not that it is His divine will for every child of God. Yes, ultimately it is His will for all to be physically whole, but not all experience it in this life.

There is a big difference between receiving eternal life, forgiveness of sins and righteousness as compared to physical healing and material blessings. You cannot put them all together in one basket. It is God's will that all be saved. But it is not God's will that all of His children enjoy divine healing and financial prosperity in this present life.

Can't Have It All Now

Contrary to popular charismatic teaching, you can't have it all now. Life in this world is not fair. This present world has sickness, decay and poverty. Jesus Christ did not die on the cross to do away with the immediate effects of sin and the fall. Ultimately, He will establish His new kingdom of physical and material blessings.

Revelation 21:4 says there will come a new heaven and a new earth where "He will wipe every tear from their eyes. There will be no more death or mourning or crying or pain, for the old order of things has passed away."

Notice the old order of things will exist until this present life is done away with. Until then there is still sickness, death, decay and tragedy. The whole earth is groaning in the pains of childbirth. We ourselves, flesh and blood, groan invariably as we *wait* eagerly for "the redemption of our bodies" (Rom. 8:18–27).

"Though outwardly we are wasting away, yet inwardly we are being renewed day by day" (2 Cor. 4:16–18). "While we are in this tent [body] we groan and are burdened, because we do not wish to be unclothed, but to be clothed with our heavenly [body] dwelling" (2 Cor. 5:4).

Life Is Not Fair

The Bible regularly speaks of life becoming fair in the end. In the end the child of God will have it all. In the end he will receive all that was promised. He will receive a glorified body. We see this truth in the words of Paul in Philippians 3:20–21: "But our citizenship is in heaven. And we eagerly await a Savior from there, the Lord Jesus Christ, who, by the power that enables him to bring everything under his control, will transform our lowly bodies so that they will be like his glorious body."

God never said He would deliver it all now to those who had the most faith. Rather, He gave every believer the "[Holy] Spirit as a deposit, guaranteeing what is to come" (2 Cor. 5:5). No believer is guaranteed divine health or healing in this present life. In this life God is more concerned about the inner spiritual qualities and character of a believer. He is more concerned about salvation, righteousness, peace, giving, self-denial, surrender, sacrifice, love, forgiveness and compassion.

Western Gospel, Not the Real Gospel

Much of what is preached as the gospel in some charismatic circles is not the gospel at all. It sounds great, but it promises something that God will not deliver. At least not totally in this life.

Western Christianity has been built upon the bigger and better, the pie in the sky, have-it-all-now, get-it-while-you-can philosophy. But Christianity for the past two thousand years has been built upon surrender, sacrifice and service. The early disciples lived sacrificial, surrendered lives. They did not live in luxury or divine health. In fact, they were persecuted, martyred and mocked. But they were glad to do it because they were "looking forward to the city with foundations, whose architect and builder is God" (Heb. 11:10).

They were not living for the here and now. If there were inconveniences, suffering and pain, so be it; they were looking forward to a better life, a life in the next world. It was not like it is today in America, where everyone is competing to have the newest revelation, the newest word from God, the answer for all of your problems, the secret for divine health and financial security. Joy and happiness in charismatic circles come from healings, miracles and revelations. Excitement comes from dynamic, positive preaching and loud, peppy music from orchestras or choirs, which all have their place. But where is the focus? The focus is on the here and now. You can receive it now. You can fight for it now. You can do spiritual warfare to bring your miracles into the here and now.

But I believe God is not so much concerned with the "here and now" as He is with the "to be later." The best is yet to come! "You ain't seen nothin' yet!" (see Rev. 21:9—22:5.) Don't look for it all now. You will get it all later. Seek Jesus, surrender your desires to Him, share the gospel with others, live in His grace and mercy. Receive His peace, joy and contentment. Let Him build the spiritual qualities of love, trust, faithfulness and service into your life now. What you need will all be yours in the next life.

Jesus Is the Focal Point

Miracles, healings and tremendous blessings are not the focal point. **Jesus is the focal point.** Being conformed to His image is the ultimate goal of the believer (Phil. 2:3–8). "For those God foreknew he also predestined to be conformed to be the likeness of his Son, that he might be the firstborn among many brothers (Rom. 8:29).

Paul Is a Model

Paul lived much of his life with suffering, pain and anguish. But because he had a proper focus he could experience true victory and joy; he was not looking for a road of physical health and financial prosperity. Look at some of his words:

"But we have this treasure in jars of clay to show that this all-surpassing power is from God and not from us. We are hard pressed on every side, but not crushed; perplexed, but not in despair; persecuted, but not abandoned; struck down, but not destroyed. We always carry around in our body the death of Jesus, so that the life of Jesus may also be revealed in our body. For we who are alive are always being given over to death for Jesus' sake, so that his life may be revealed in our mortal body. So then, death is at work in us, but life is at work in you" (2 Cor. 4:7–12).

"Are they servants of Christ? (I am out of my mind to talk like this.) I am more. I have worked much harder, been in prison more frequently, been flogged more severely, and been exposed to death again and again. Five times I received from the Jews the forty lashes minus one. Three times I was beaten with rods, once I was stoned, three times I was shipwrecked, I spent a night and a day in the open sea, I have been constantly on the move. I have been in danger from rivers, in danger from bandits, in danger from my own countrymen, in danger from Gentiles; in danger in the city, in danger in the country, in danger at sea; and in danger from false brothers. I have labored and toiled and have often gone without sleep; I have known hunger and thirst and have often gone without food; I have been cold and naked. Besides everything else, I face daily the pressure of my concern for all the churches. Who is weak, and I do not feel weak? Who is led into sin, and I do not inwardly burn?

"If I must boast, I will boast of the things that show my weakness. The God and Father of the Lord Jesus, who is to be praised forever, knows that I am not lying. In Damascus the governor under King Aretas had the city of the Damascenes guarded in order to arrest me. But I was lowered in a basket from a window in the wall and slipped through his hands.

"I must go on boasting. Although there is nothing to be gained, I will go on to visions and revelations from the Lord. I know a man in Christ who fourteen years ago was caught up to the third heaven. Whether it was in the body or out of the body I do not know—God knows. And I know that this man—whether in the body or apart from the body I do not know, but God knows—was caught up to paradise. He heard inexpressible things, things that man is not permitted to tell. I will boast about a man like that, but I will not boast about myself, except about my weaknesses. Even if I should choose to boast, I would not be a fool, because I would be speaking the truth. But I refrain, so no one will think more of me than is warranted by what I do or say. To keep me from becoming conceited because of these surpassingly great revelations, there was given me a thorn in my flesh, a messenger of Satan, to torment me. Three times I pleaded with the Lord to take it away from me. But he said to me, 'My grace is sufficient for you, for my power is made perfect in weakness.' Therefore I will boast all the more gladly about my weaknesses so that Christ's power may rest on me. That is why, for Christ's sake, I delight in weaknesses, in insults, in hardships, in persecutions, in difficulties. For when I am weak, then I am strong" (2 Cor. 11:23—12:10).

"But even if I am being poured out like a drink offering on the sacrifice and service coming from your faith, I am glad and rejoice with all of you" (Phil. 2:17).

"For I am already being poured out like a drink offering, and the time has come for my departure. I have fought the good fight, I have finished the race, I have kept the faith. Now there is in store for me the crown of righteousness, which the Lord, the righteous Judge, will award to me on that day—and not only to me, but also to all who have longed for his appearing" (2 Tim. 4:6–8).

"I rejoice greatly in the Lord that at last you have renewed your concern for me. Indeed, you have been concerned, but you had no opportunity to show it. I am not saying this because I am in need, for I have learned to be content whatever the circumstances. I know what it is to be in need, and I know what it is to have plenty. I have learned the secret of being content in any and every situation, whether well fed or hungry, whether living in plenty or in want. I can do everything through him who gives me strength" (Phil. 4:10–13).

"But whatever was to my profit I now consider loss for the sake of Christ. What is more, I consider everything a loss compared to the surpassing greatness of knowing Christ Jesus my Lord, for whose sake I have lost all things. I consider them rubbish, that I may gain Christ and be found in him, not having a righteousness of my own that comes from the law, but that which is through faith in Christ—the righteousness that comes from God and is by faith. I want to know Christ and the power of his resurrection and the fellowship of sharing in his sufferings, becoming like him in his death, and so, somehow, to attain to the resurrection from the dead.

"Not that I have already obtained all this, or have already been made perfect, but I press on to take hold of that for which Christ Jesus took hold of me. Brothers, I do not consider myself yet to have taken hold of it. But one thing I do: Forgetting what is behind and straining toward what is ahead, I press on toward the goal to win the prize for which God has called me heavenward in Christ Jesus" (Phil. 3:7–14).

Notice that Paul's focus is Jesus Christ. It is pouring himself out for the Lord. The focus of the gospel is not physical or material. Listen to Paul's words in 1 Timothy 6:6–12, 17–19: "But godliness with contentment is great gain. For we brought nothing into the world, and we can take nothing out of it. But if we have food and clothing, we will be content with that. People who want to get rich fall into temptation and a trap and into many foolish and harmful desires that plunge men into ruin and destruction. For the love of money is a root of all kinds of evil. Some people, eager for money, have wandered from the faith and pierced themselves with many griefs.

"But you, man of God, flee from all this, and pursue righteousness, godliness, faith, love, endurance and gentleness. Fight the good fight of the faith. Take hold of the eternal life to which you were called when you made your good confession in the presence of many witnesses.

"Command those who are rich in this present world not to be arrogant nor to put their hope in wealth, which is so uncertain, but to put their hope in God, who richly provides us with everything for our enjoyment. Command them to do good, to be rich in good deeds, and to be generous and willing to share. In this way they will lay up treasure for themselves as a firm foundation for the coming age, so that they may take hold of the life that is truly life."

More to Healing Than Compassion

There is more to divine healing than God's compassion. He does not enjoy seeing any of His children suffer physical disease, but God's purpose outweighs His compassion. Often God denies comfort for a greater purpose. Consider Job, who experienced tremendous pain at the permission of a compassionate God. God's full compassion will not ultimately be experienced by the believer until total healing comes in the next life.

Some believe one major reason Jesus came to earth was to heal the sick compassionately. But a closer look at the Gospels will show that many of Jesus' miracles were for a greater purpose than to relieve physical suffering. Most of His miracles of healing took place to show others He truly was the Christ. If He came to heal everyone out of compassion, why didn't He literally speak the word and heal every sick person in the region of Israel? Instead, He healed people along His way to reveal who He was.

That is why Jesus could leave multitudes still sick and suffering in John 5:1–14 and heal only one man, why He could turn other sick and afflicted away as Luke 5:15–16 says: "Yet the news about him spread all the more, so that crowds of people came to hear him and to be healed of their sicknesses. But Jesus often withdrew to lonely places and prayed."

Contrary to some teaching, Jesus did not heal everyone who came to Him. Yes, there are some instances like that of the centurion (Matt. 8:5ff.), the Syrophoenician woman (Mark 7:24ff.), the woman with the hemorrhage (Mark 5:25–34) and others whose faith moved Jesus to heal them. With God, there is variation.

Here, There or in the Air

Therefore, *'til healing comes*, whether here, there or in the air, the follower of Christ has the victory knowing that "in all these things we are more than conquerors through him who loved us.

"For I am convinced that neither death nor life, neither angels, nor demons, neither the present nor the future, nor any powers, neither height nor depth, nor anything else in all creation, will be able to separate us from the love of God that is in Christ Jesus our Lord" (Rom. 8:37–39).

Jesus told Pilate that His kingdom was not of this world (see John 18:36). In this current earthly kingdom there is sin, sickness and satanic influence. That is what the Bible calls "the old order of things." Believers are not of this world. They have different priorities and values. Sure, physical comfort and financial success are natural to strive for. But they are not necessary in order to have a victorious and fulfilled life. The believer's victory is in Christ, not in circumstances. Therefore, *'til healing comes*, the true, genuine follower of Jesus is "more than a conqueror."

It is important to realize that we do not experience in this life all the kingdom of God offers. It is not essential that we do. Since Jesus' kingdom is not of this world, the believer can stand confidently on hope and expect that the best is yet to come.

A day is coming when all the saints of God will walk the streets of gold. Every believer will receive his resurrection body. "In a flash, in the twinkling of an eye, at the last trumpet. For the trumpet will sound, the dead will be raised imperishable, and we will be changed. For the perishable must clothe itself with the imperishable, and the mortal with immortality. When the perishable has been clothed with the imperishable, and the mortal with immortality, then the saying that is written will come true, "Death has been swallowed up in victory. Where, O death, is your victory? Where, O death, is your sting?'" (1 Cor. 15:52–55).

Remember the Old Hymns

What a glorious day that will be! The believer will live in a body that will never experience decay, disease or death. There will be no more cancer, heart disease, birth defects, polio, muscular dystrophy or multiple sclerosis. No more handicaps or disabilities, no more wheelchairs, iron lungs or ventilators.

At the marriage supper of the Lamb we can eat high-fat, high-cholesterol, high-sodium foods. Praise God, you won't have to diet, jog or exercise any longer.

I love the words of those old hymns:
> What a day that will be when my Jesus I shall see,
> and I look upon His face, the One who saved me by His grace,
> when He takes me by the hand, and leads me to the Promised Land, what a day, glorious day that will be.[1]

and...

One glad morning when this life is o'er, I'll fly
   away.
To a home on God's celestial shore, I'll fly away.
I'll fly away O glory, I'll fly away.
When I die, hallelujah, by and by, I'll fly away.[2]

Heavenly Expectations, Out of This World

Those of us who suffer from chronic illness can receive joy and hope as we look forward to the glories of heaven. Looking forward to heaven can make the long roads of this life more bearable, can help us handle those terrible medical tests, radical surgeries, chemotherapy and chronic pain.

This life with its fluctuations between times of great joy and times of great sorrow will all balance out when we look at everything through the eyes of eternity. Life can have its silver linings and its dark clouds, but one thing for sure, "there shall be no more curse: but the throne of God and of the Lamb shall be in it; and his servants shall serve him: And they shall see his face: and his name shall be in their foreheads. And there shall be no night there; and they need no candle, neither light of the sun; for the Lord God giveth them light, and they shall reign for ever and ever" (Rev. 22:3–5, KJV).

A time is coming with healing for every saint of God. The glorious, miraculous healing that will be final. A healing beyond all earthly healings. The final healing and ultimate restoration.

I look forward to a day when I will have a whole and perfect body. It will be great to look at myself and see two perfect arms, two perfect legs. I'll be able to stand up straight with a perfect spine. "No more tears, no more death, neither sorrow, nor crying, nor pain" (see Rev. 21:4).

The Best Is Yet to Come

Truly the best is yet to come when every child of God will be able to say, "My ultimate healing finally came."

'Til healing comes, keep looking up.

Notes

Chapter I

1. Calvin and Arminius were theologians during the sixteenth century. Calvin magnified the sovereignty of God along with the doctrine of election, predestination and providence, while Arminius magnified man's free will and his personal responsibilities and actions.

2. Henry Clarence Theissen, *Introductory Lectures in Systematic Theology* (William B. Eerdmans Publishing Co., 1949., 15th printing 1975), p. 119.

3. *Ibid.*, p. 120.

4. *Ibid.*, p. 122.

5. *Ibid.*, p. 128.
6. *Ibid.*, p. 129.
7. *Ibid.*, p. 147.

Chapter II

1. Many who teach that it is God's will and a believer's right to be healed any time faith is applied and a proper way of thinking and confessing is appropriated are referred to as "word of faith" or "hyper-faith" teachers. Some of the more popular speakers and authors are: Kenneth Hagin Sr., *Seven Things You Should Know About Divine Healing* (Rhemus Bible Church, 1979); Kenneth Copeland, *You Are Healed* (Fort Worth, TX: Kenneth Copeland Ministries, 1987); Gloria Copeland, *And Jesus Healed Them All* (Fort Worth, TX: Kenneth Copeland Ministries, 1981); T.L. Osborn, *Healing the Sick* (Tulsa, OK: Harrison House Pub.); Dr. Fredrick K.C. Price, *How Faith Works* (Tulsa, OK: Harrison House Pub., 1976); F.F. Bosworth, *Christ the Healer* (Dallas, TX); Smith Wigglesworth, *The Apostle of Faith* (Springfield, MO: Frodsham GPH).

2. Fredrick K.C. Price, *Is Healing For All?* (Tulsa, OK: Harrison House Publishing, 1976.).

Chapter III

1. George Eldon Ladd, *A Theology of the New Testament*, (Grand Rapids, MI: Wm. B. Eerdmans, 1974), p. 364–365. Here Ladd speaks about salvation being present and eschatological.

2. *Ibid.*, p. 551–552. The phrase "now and not yet" is alluded to when Ladd says, "He (the believer) has already experienced the new life, but he looks forward to the inheritance of eternal life. He has already been saved, but he is still awaiting his salvation."

3. George Eldon Ladd, *The Gospel of the Kingdom*

(Grand Rapids, MI: Wm. B. Eerdmans Pub. Co., 1959), p. 69.

4. Dr. Charles Farah Jr., *From the Pinnacle of the Temple* (Plainfield, NJ: Logos International Pub. Co.), p. 35–36.

5. P.C. Nelson, *Bible Doctrines* (Springfield, MO: Gospel Publishing House), p. 96.

6. Nelson, p. 97–98.

7. G. Raymond Carlson, *Our Faith and Fellowship* (Springfield, MO: Gospel Publishing House), p. 95

8. Carlson, p. 98.

9. "Divine Healing — An Integral Part of the Gospel" (Springfield, MO: A 1974 position paper issued by the Assemblies of God General Council through Gospel Publishing House) 6-7 (Gospel Publishing House also has a helpful position paper called "The Believer and Positive Confession").

10. *Ibid*, p. 9–10.

11. *The Gospel of the Kingdom*, p. 76–79.

Chapter IV

1. Michael Horton, *The Agony of Deceit* (Chicago: Moody Press, 1990). D.R. McConnell, *A Different Gospel* (Peabody, MA: Hendrickson Publishers, 1988).

2. W.E. Vine, *An Expository Dictionary of New Testament Words* (Old Tappan, NJ Revell Co., 1966), p. 401, 402.

3. B.J. Willhite, *Why Pray?* (Altamonte Springs, FL: Creation House Pub., 1988) p. 59–60.

4. *Ibid.*, p. 136–137.

5. *Ibid.*, p. 138–140.

6. *Ibid.*, p. 59–60.

Chapter V

1. Some resource books on the gifts of the Spirit are: Donald Gee, *Spiritual Gifts* (Springfield, MO:

Notes

Gospel Publishing House) and Dr. Stanley Horton, *The Holy Spirit* (Springfield, MO: Gospel Publishing House).

2. Sometimes sin can be the cause of illness as a judgment or curse from God for disobedience. A number of popular charismatic teachers magnify the results that can happen from a curse on the family line to the third or fourth generation. I feel much of this is over-simplified and magnified by trying to pin down too much illness due to a curse. but it can be the result in certain instances. There is a classic charismatic book written by Derek Prince, *Blessings and Cursings* (Old Tappan, NJ: Revell, Chosen Books). Prince expounds in an exhaustive fashion what many charismatic teachers believe about curses and how to break them. I do not subscribe to the author's conclusions entirely, but some of what he says is possible. Anyone wishing to cover the base of what sin and curses can do should read this book.

3. What Satan and demons can do is a very broad topic. Helpful books for further study are by Martin I. Brubeck, *The Adversary* (Chicago: Moody Press, 1975) and Merrill F. Unger, *Demons in the World Today* (Wheaton: Tyndale House Pub., 1971).

Chapter VI

1. Paul Yonggi Cho, *Suffering, Why Me?* (South Plainfield, NJ: Bridge Publishing Inc., 1986), p. 100.

2. *Ibid.*, p. 101.

3. *Ibid.*, p. 99.

4. *Ibid.*, p. 96.

5. *Ibid.*, p. 94.

6. *Ibid.*, p. 97.

7. *Ibid.*, p. 102–103.

8. C.S. Lewis, *The Problem of Pain* (New York: The Macmillan Co., 1962), p. 93, 95–97.

9. *Ibid.*, p. 110.

Chapter VII
1. *The Thompson Chain Reference Bible*, NIV (The B.B. Kirkbride Bible Co. and Zondervan 1983), p. 1406.
2. Joni Eareckson Tada, *Joni* (Zondervan, 1976). (Also see Joni's book *A Step Further* by Zondervan Pub. House.).

Chapter VIII
1. Jamie Buckingham, *A Summer of Miracles* (Altamonte Springs, FL: Creation House, 1991).
2. Jamie Buckingham, *Daughter of Destiny* (Plainfield, NJ: Logos Pub).

Chapter IX
1. James Hill, "What a Day That Will Be," c. 1955 Ben L. Speer.
2. Albert E. Brumley, "I'll Fly Away," c. 1932 in "Wonderful Message" by Hartford Music Co., 1960 by Albert E. Brumley and Sons.

Selected Bibliography

Barron, Bruce. *The Health & Wealth Gospel.* Downers Grove, Illinois: InterVarsity Press, 1987.

Billheimer, Paul E. *Don't Waste Your Sorrows.* Fort Washington, Pennsylvania: Christian Literature Crusade Inc., 1977.

Cho, Paul Yonggi. *Suffering, Why Me?* South Plainfield, New Jersey: Bridge Publishing, Inc., 1986.

Dobson, James. *When God Doesn't Make Sense.* Wheaton, Illinois; Tyndale Publishers, 1993.

Farah, Charles Jr., Ph.D. *From the Pinnacle of the Temple.* Plainfield, New Jersey: Logos International.

Hanegraaff, Hank. *Christianity in Crisis.* Eugene, Oregon: Harvest House Publishers, 1993.

Horton, Michael. *The Agony of Deceit.* Chicago: Moody Press, 1990.

Hunt, Dave. *Beyond Seduction.* Eugene, Oregon: Harvest House Publishers, 1987.

Hunt, Dave, and T.A. McMahon. *The Seduction of Christianity.* Eugene, Oregon: Harvest House Publishers, 1985.

Jeter, Hugh. *By His Stripes.* Springfield, Missouri. Gospel Publishing House.

Ladd, George Eldon. *A Theology of the New Testament.* Grand Rapids, Michigan: William B. Eerdmans Publishing Company, 1974.

McConnell, D.R. *A Different Gospel.* Peabody, Massachusetts: Hendrickson Publishers, 1988.

Pardington, George P., Ph.D. *Outline Studies in Christian Doctrine.* Harrisburg, Pennsylvania: Christian Alliance Publishing Company, 1926.

Pearlman, Myer. *Knowing the Doctrines of the Bible.* Springfield, Missouri: Gospel Publishing House, 1937.

Strong, Augustus Hopkins, D.D., L.L.D. *Systematic Theology.* Old Tappan, New Jersey: Fleming H. Revell Company, 1907.

Thiessen, Henry C. *Lectures in Systematic Theology.* Grand Rapids, Michigan: William B. Eerdmans Publishing Company, 1949.

Whitworth, Robert Lee. *God Told Me to Tell You.* Green Forest, Arkansas: New Leaf Press, 1988.

Willhite, B.J. *Why Pray?* Altamonte Springs, Florida: Creation House, 1988.

Wimber, John, and Kevin Springer. *Power Healing.* San Francisco, California: Harper & Row, 1987.

Wise, Robert L. *When There Is No Miracle.* Ventura, California: Regal Books, 1977.

Wright, Gordon. *In Quest of Healing.* Springfield, Missouri: Gospel Publishing House, 1978.

About the Author

Kenneth Dignan is an ordained minister with the Assemblies of God and is president and founder of 'Til Healing Comes Ministries. This evangelistic ministry was established to provide teaching and resources on the balance of faith, which is so necessary in understanding the biblical principles of suffering and divine healing.

Ken has become a popular speaker at conferences, seminars, churches, retreats and schools. He also serves on the pastoral staff of a local church and resides in the Chicagoland area with his wife, Joni, and four sons: Andy, Patrick, Ryan and Britt.

He has recorded a gospel music tape, produced a video series on the topic of divine healing and appears regularly on WCFC-TV, the Christian station in Chicago.

To schedule Rev. Dignan to speak or for information on his book, tapes and resources, address your request to:

'Til Healing Comes Ministries
6330 W. 127th Street
Palos Heights, IL 60463
(708) 385-2770